A Sweet Life in Homemaking

A Decade of Thrift, Frugality, and Homemaking

By Kate Singh

Author of *The Homemade Housewife, The Frugal Life,* and *One Paycheck and a Housewife*

Edited by Perla Thornwood

Cover design by James at www.goonwrite.com

Kate's YouTube Channel: Coffee With Kate

Kate's blog: www.coffeewithkate.blog or www.katesinghsite.com

Table of Contents

Chapter 1 Homemaking

Chapter 2 Nesting and Finding Our True Home

Chapter 3 The Healing Effects of Family

Chapter 4 My Personal Grocery Store and Café

Chapter 5 How Frugal Living Launched a Writing Career

Chapter 6 Homesteading in Town

Chapter 7 When You Have Very Little Money to Work With

Chapter 8 Decorating With Little or No Money

Chapter 9 Marriage, Motherhood, Being at Home, and Modern Society

Chapter 10 The Zen Home

Chapter 11 How to Build a Home and Life on a Small Budget

Chapter 12 My Past Writings to Inspire

Chapter 13 Home Cooking

Chapter 1

Homemaking

I sit here this morning, beginning this book not knowing if I will ever publish it, but I just love this topic so much that I could talk about it every day (and I do). It's not that I'm a dull soul who only ponders my chores and ways to save a nickel. No; I just look about and see this life that is so cozy and pleasing, so charming and delicious, and I want everyone to experience it, to know that a fulfilling and truly joy-filled life is right there for us all and it doesn't cost a fortune. It only requires creativity, some hard work in the beginning, thinking outside the box, and being willing to give up the mainstream life.

Did I always want to be a housewife? Yes, I did. I also wanted to be an interior decorator, a psychologist, a writer, an actress, and a secretary. And I'm all of those things today.

This very morning I sit and work in my office, at my large desk, enjoying a steamy latte, while my coworkers are busy with their own projects of studying and art.

I sit at my long dining room table in our tiny dining room. I am wearing my nightgown, sipping a latte I made using an Italian stovetop espresso maker and a handheld milk frother that has changed my mornings into something beautiful. My two little boys create art using a coffee can filled with colored pens from last Christmas and scratch paper from Dad's gas station reports. They look up information about dinosaurs on the little Chromebook that we all share and use for our individual projects, research, and continued learning.

A small Presto Heat Dish heats up the living room, and when that room is toasty enough, I move it to the dining room. Pandora is on the generic Smart TV in the living room, playing all the many stations I've created over the years. Music is big in this house. Our days consist of listening to music, drinking coffee, drawing, learning, and writing.

I have chosen to raise my family off the main path. However, we are not living in the hills and off the grid with compostable toilets and kerosene lamps. As much as I love the old-fashioned way of living, I also love modern convenience.

When I was a little girl, I was a big fan of *Little House on The Prairie* and read every book until it fell apart. I even read some literature written by Rose Wilder Lane, Laura's daughter. I was obsessed with pioneers and spent hours sketching log cabins and pioneer mothers hanging laundry on rope clothes lines while babies rolled around in vegetable gardens.

Today I live in an old 1941 stucco in the old part of a small town. I hang my clothes on the line outside and my front yard and backyard are filled with fruit and nut trees and kitchen gardens. My babies are now 5 and 7 years old.

I see that times fluctuate with our economy, and have already observed a large and mighty recession back in 2008. Although many people suffered during this time, I did not because I had nothing to begin with. I also remember the dot-com era. What I learned from both times is that simple is better and to stay the heck out of the rat race called modern living.

Getting married and becoming a housewife were the biggest blessings I have been rewarded with, but they didn't come to me until much later in life. I had experienced the hustle and bustle of nine-to-five jobs, with long commutes into the city. When I got married at age 40 and became pregnant with my first son, I was in heaven. When I "retired" from the office to stay home, I started a celebration that is going even stronger today.

I've always wanted to be home. I love home. I love all that is my daily housework, cooking, and baking. I can sit here and sip homemade coffee drinks and listen to my children chat over their little life theories. I am home to boil bone broth for my old dogs and to throw toy chickens and balls for the new addition, a Dachshund pup named Molly. All are rescues and all are smart, adorable dogs.

Being home, I have the time to create ambiance and charm for my family. There are always hot meals ready to be served along with the wonderful smell of freshly baked bread. Something is always simmering and baking in the kitchen.

Being home, I can grow lots of food and learn the craft of canning and preserving it. This saves us a lot of money and ensures that my family eats clean, organic, fresh food without any chemicals, dyes, or additives; just herbs, salt and maybe a squeeze of fresh lemon juice.

Being home means that everyone is in a safe and nurturing environment. It means that my husband returns from the outside world to good smells, good food, and comfort.

My being home means that no one is ever lonely because Mama is home to comfort, listen, cook, talk, and play. Mama is here filling the home with delightful aromas, noise, activity, chores, music, and light.

I can usually be found in the kitchen working over a new recipe or filling my bulk jars and organizing my shelves. If I'm not in the kitchen, you can peek out into the living room or my bedroom and I'll likely be sitting next to a pile of clothes, folding slowly, while I watch a sitcom, getting in my daily dose of laughter. You can also find me here, typing away at my laptop working on a book or my blog.

For me, being home has brought gifts beyond enjoying babies. It has also brought the deliciousness and joy of homemaking. I have had time to build a writing career and create a YouTube channel and a blog. These have been wonderful creative outlets and have also become a source of income. The small royalties help to make ends meet and give us a bit of wiggle room. They allow for special classes for my boys as well as store-bought organics. I have found a huge life in homemaking.

Being a housewife and/or stay-at-home mom can be a lonely job that feels like domestic drudgery at times. Some women and men detest this life. I get it. It is a hard job and you either love it or you don't. I have days when I feel isolated, when I wake up exhausted at the mere thought of doing dishes and wiping down counters five times a day, making beds, sweeping floors, and cooking the same dishes. It's like the movie *Groundhog Day* starring Bill Murray. Same day over and over and over!

But there is a trick to this life and it isn't just surviving it. You can thrive in it, love it!

Surrender and dive in deep. Make it a game. Florence Scovel Shinn wrote a small book called *The Game of Life*. It is about metaphysics and creating the life you desire. Some frugalists will say, "Make money-saving into a game." I say, "Make it all a game." This is especially important when we are broke and living on very little money. The other night I watched a movie and the protagonist said, "Life is a game. Have fun." I agree wholeheartedly.

Life, work, saving money, cleaning … everything is a game to be played, to be enjoyed. I have found a way to really enjoy years of doing the same work. I have learned the craft of making the same routines and chores fresh and new over and over again. I have learned to challenge myself with the saving of household funds and creating new ways to keep house. I change menus, try new dishes, and rearrange the house to make the day new.

Writing has been a wonderful escape. When I tire of the same old thing, I sit at my laptop and express myself, share my life, or escape into a fictional life. I would never have entered the world of writing if I didn't have the privilege of staying home.

My heart is full of appreciation and gratitude for my husband who goes out each day and works in this busy world without one word of complaint. He provides well for his family, works hard, and is devoted and loyal. Because of this, I am well taken care of and protected from the things in the world that I don't enjoy. I can reside safely and joyfully at home to nest and focus on our children.

To honor the gift my husband has given us, I, in return, have built a home filled with color, comfort, and good vibrations. I've learned to cook well and manage our money wisely. We both do our jobs well and have built a good life together. That is what companions do. They build good lives and raise happy children together.

Chapter 2

Nesting and Finding Our True Home

We live in a small blue cottage in an older neighborhood and are within walking distance of everything, depending on how far you want to walk. This is the first home my husband and I have ever owned, and we take not one inch of it for granted. It took many years of hard work and scrimping and saving each penny to earn this house.

When I was a little girl, I had a large, plain Victorian dollhouse that my mother bought me one year. It was sort of "build-it-yourself," with the main house pre-assembled, but you had to paint it and decorate the interior with wallpaper, rugs, and curtains. Back then, antique dollhouse furniture was very popular and everywhere you went, there would be a small section of the store dedicated to little velvet chaise lounges, glossy wood dining tables, and tiny china tea sets. I collected a piece everywhere I went.

But I believe the dollhouse I had the most fun with was a homemade one. My mother had a friend whose daughter was very creative. She taught me how to make a dollhouse from two boxes stacked on each other. You could paint it and cut out windows and glue pieces of fabric for curtains. I used old wrapping paper as wallpaper and cut up old blankets or clothing for rugs and bedding. Empty egg cartons would be converted into living room chairs and couches, strawberry baskets became cribs, and acorn tops were transformed into bowls and cups. This was the most fun.

The dollhouses were lost and destroyed over time, but I have that memory. I have always been one to decorate every room I've ever had, every studio, apartment, or house. No matter where I lived, I would scrub, wash, and decorate my space. However, after a couple of decades of renting, I did lose some of that enthusiasm. Landlords can be a bit of a crimp on creativity. "Don't plant trees!" "I would prefer it if you didn't dig up the lawn for a garden." "No, white walls are how they need to stay." So boring.

When Bali and I got married, we spent hundreds of dollars painting the master bedroom, only to move a couple of months later. In the next house, we wanted to have a garden and a beautiful yard, so we spent thousands on it. We moved a year later.

By the next house, Bali put a cap on how much energy and money we would put into a rental. "We do all the work, spend all the money, and then we leave, and they reap the benefits!" He was right. I kept it simple with the last two rentals. I just made the home clean and cozy and decorated with things we could pack up and take with us.

And now we have our own little cottage in town. It's my very first grown-up dollhouse and I've had so much fun painting all the rooms in different colors, filling up every inch of ground with my favorite fruit and nut trees, and learning to grow everything I normally buy in the store. My home and yard are beautiful and productive.

I've learned a lot from other people's homes and yards. It was when we lived in Fort Bragg, California that I got the idea to really utilize the yard. We had a Latino family who lived down the street and when I went for walks, I would peek over their fence. They had gardens, chickens, a coop, a greenhouse, compost pile, cacti, and even some fruit vines growing along the fences. They were all crammed into a small yard. Every inch was being used to grow food and raise chickens. Food was grown on fences and in pots on the porch. It was the first time I had seen a yard that wasn't made up of just a lawn and flowers, it was made to feed and serve the family. I loved the idea and grew a small garden that year, but only harvested a basket of goods. It isn't so easy to grow food on the coast, unless you are very much into leafy greens. Those grow wonderfully in the fog.

When we bought this house, we began planting apple and orange trees in the backyard and pomegranate and avocado trees in the front yard. We started out with a few raised beds and eventually we just dug up the whole backyard and fenced it in. I had been watching YouTube videos of people growing food in their front yards and I agreed that the lawn was useless and a waste of energy with all the mowing and watering. I was inspired by the Dervaes family who crammed a whole farm into their 4,000 sq. ft. yard in a Los Angeles neighborhood, as well as Jake Mace, The Vegan Athlete, who grew 200 fruit trees and 20 raised beds in his Arizona backyard just by using a ton of mulch to make the soil rich.

As for nesting, well, I have had more fun with this little house. It's only 1,065 sq. ft. and has two bedrooms, but I've managed to rearrange it every which way. Below the hideous, stained, beige carpet we found beautiful, old wood floors that we brought back to life with a couple of generous layers of Scott's Liquid Gold. Every room is painted a different, cheerful color and I wouldn't have it any other way.

It doesn't cost much to make a home look fantastic. Paint and a deep cleaning are a marvelous cure for what ails the house. If you have an old house, say from the 1800s to early 1900s, you may be lucky and have old wood floors, too. You don't need to go through all the drama of sanding and varnishing. It might not be a good idea to sand old floors as they may become too thin. All you need to do is scrub them well. We used a bucket of hot water, strong soap, and stainless steel scrubbers. The water turned black the first couple of times. After you've gotten the dirt and grime off, use the Scott's Liquid Gold. Alternatively, you can let the floors dry for 24 hours and use something more powerful such as Rejuvenate All Floors Restorer. Both products can be found at your local hardware store such as Home Depot or Lowe's. Walmart may even carry them.

To the windows, we added nice, sturdy white blinds — the faux wood kind, not the cheap kind that you find in apartments. In retrospect, I probably should have just bought curtains. They are more attractive and elegant, and you can get the thick flannel ones that keep the cold out at night. This would have been much cheaper and easier. The blinds were about $30 or $40 each.

We hired a handyman to help with a few projects, but Bali and I did mostly everything by hand. In the end, everything cost less than $20,000. That included building a nice wooden six-foot fence all the way around our property, a white picket fence in the front yard, exterior paint, a few coats of lead paint sealant throughout the inside of the whole house just a safety precaution since it's an older house, then painting each room a special color.

We also had some plumbing and electrical work done, disposed of all the old carpet and lining, and had tile installed in the kitchen and laundry room. There was also the purchase of a new garage door, some fruit and nut trees, soil, wood and bricks for raised garden beds, and grape vines.

If we were to do it over we would do it all ourselves, build simpler fences, install linoleum in the kitchen, leave the exterior paint as is (it didn't really need it), and I would have planted the gardens in the ground instead of starting off in beds and having to buy expensive soil. I would have put more thought into where to plant our trees. I would have only purchased these from a reputable and local nursery instead of Lowe's and Home Depot. All that would have saved us $10,000!

My point is that it doesn't take that much to make a fixer-upper look lovely again. However, planning and thinking things through is key.

The Daily Grind of Cleaning and Keeping House

Over the summer, I was feeling a bit wilty, and housework was wearing on me. I began studying minimalism vlogs and documentaries with great interest. There are so many channels on YouTube that specialize or focus on organizing, but one I found particularly fun is *ClutterBug*. Cas, the content creator, came up with a 12-week challenge called, "Hug Your

Home." She provides a schedule to help guide you in tackling a certain room in your home each week, which is to be completely decluttered, clean, and organized. I spent the next few months hauling bags and boxes to local thrift stores.

I would sit with my coffee mug and watch *Minimalism: A Documentary About the Important Things* on Netflix. I could relate with the idea of putting a stop to mindless consuming. What really resonated with me was when one of the producers, Ryan Nicodemus, talked about always wanting and waiting for that next thing, the next product or item, and the next paycheck. It's an empty existence. It made sense to me that instead of focusing on these things, it would be better to want and have less – less stuff, less wanting, less spending, and more of doing and having the things that are truly rich in life, such as family time, being out enjoying nature, and traveling.

At that time, I had been visiting my chiropractor often to help relieve the soreness from not only all the deep cleaning I had been doing, but from all the hauling and pushing of heavy furniture to the other side of the room (I like to rearrange my home often to give it a new look and feel). I was tired of all the hours of endless cleaning and organizing.

So, I purged the easy stuff first. It's not so hard to rid your house of broken or ugly things. It's easy to go into the closet and remove all the stained, torn, and worn out clothing. Then you get rid of stuff that doesn't make you feel happy looking at it. This may sound silly, but it is true. Everything holds a vibration. I had a lovely red recliner that my neighbor gave me, but it was painted leather and every time it touched my lovely butter yellow walls (and it somehow always did, no matter how far away I moved it), it left ugly, red streaks. I passed it on to a few bachelors who were thrilled to have it. I had another recliner that we adored but the foot part broke and it was forever crippled and lopsided. That one went to one of our neighbors. I had paintings that didn't evoke a feeling of peace or admiration. They were just covering the walls. Off they went to the thrift store.

When I had trouble getting rid of a certain item, it helped to remember that there is someone out there who will use it to its full potential and love it dearly. Meanwhile, the item was just sitting alone in our house, unused, and collecting dust. Free your stuff! Give your stuff the chance to be used and loved.

Some things took weeks to part with. Other pieces wound up in the garage. Sometimes it's best to set items aside when on a cleaning frenzy. I have shipped things off to Goodwill only to need them a year later. There are many items I can think of that I need today, but gave away ages ago. One can store a few things in the garage without being considered a hoarder.

Over that summer of purging and organizing the house deeply, I woke up one morning with the itch to move. I wanted to move to a town up the hill in the mountains because it calls to me. Now that some time has passed, I look back and see that I was also trying to "move" out some old feelings, and it turns out that running is my old trick.

To some, purging and decluttering is just that, simply cleaning things out. But I believe it to be an act of emotional purging and decluttering as well. Everything holds energy, and as we haul truckloads off to the thrift store for others to find and put to good use, we are letting go of old energy . . . maybe other people's old energy? We are letting go of a past or situation that doesn't serve us. We are moving out clutter that keeps us stuck. We are making room for new and different things. As we transform our homes and surroundings, we are also working on the inside transformation. The outside reflects the inside.

We recently found a mobile home on two acres of land that we wanted to purchase. The deal was that we would sell our home to put a large down payment on it. Our house went on the market and boy, was that a flurry of activity. We weeded and cleared out the gardens, repainted doors and walls, treated the floors with Scott's Liquid Gold, and polished the whole house to shine.

Our realtor as well as several wise ladies on my YouTube channel suggested I really clear out my décor to give the house a simple, stripped down look. That is when I really experienced a minimalist home. All I had was furniture. Everything was packed up and in the garage: all my photos, paintings, knick-knacks, candles, and books. I *will* say that it became very quick and easy to clean the house. It was also drab and depressing.

When things fell through with the land purchase and we took the house off the market, I brought everything back in from the garage. I then went out to Home Depot and purchased two shelving units. I used the larger one in my handcrafted pantry so that I could really build up our food storage. The smaller one went in the dining room to hold all of our books, candles, photos, and plants.

One afternoon, I was at my dentist's office waiting room. I picked up an AD (Architectural Digest) magazine and began browsing through it. I expected to find lots of sterile-looking "modern" rooms decorated with shiny plastic chairs, polished stainless steel, and cold granite countertops. Instead, I was joyfully greeted by pages filled with beautiful colors, layers, and textures. I saw photos of gorgeous antiques and embroidered silks.

Nothing matched, and everything was draped with brightly colored cloth and stacked with vibrant pillows. Paintings covered the walls and side dressers were loaded with china and silver ornaments. Too much was not enough.

I was inspired and emboldened. It was in style to be shabby chic, to choose throw pillows that didn't even come close to matching, and to have a charmingly cluttered room. This spoke to me.

Being that we were on a budget, I took $100 from the coffers and promptly ran to Goodwill. The thrift stores in my town are a bit dirty and lacking but I had hope. I did well, filling my cart with prettily patterned cloth, colorful pillows, cozy throws, and charming paintings. I rushed back home with my loot, washed everything, and began decorating just like the magazine showed me. I was missing a few million dollars in my budget to do as the professional decorators in the magazine had done, but I had so much fun, and my house is very colorful and lively to this day.

Finding Our Nest

How did we find this little stucco house in a small town? First, I will be honest in admitting that this town was not even on my top 20 list of choices, and this house was the last (and I mean *last*) house that I bid on or even wanted to bid on. I only bid on this small house to play the game of bidding on two or more houses at once in order to increase my chances of success. I had already been outbid by a few coins on several houses and I was in it to win it!

And I did. I started the bidding on this run-down HUD (U.S. Department of Housing and Urban Development) house, and the next morning I was the proud parent of a little home that was once overrun by squatters, drug dealers, and one prostitute.

The reason I gave into this small town surrounded by rice fields and walnut orchards was as silly as a movie. Well, that and the reality that it was the only town left that had affordable housing in our area.

When we were on the hunt for a house, I watched Disney's *McFarland, USA* one afternoon. The story is about a coach who winds up in a tiny, dusty farm community coaching at a mostly Latino high school. It is the story of overcoming all odds; of kids coming from hardship and poverty and succeeding with the support of their families, strong passions, and a drive. All the boys came from families of immigrant workers who struggled, but they thrived on the track and went on to have a winning running team, eventually making it to college and having successful careers.

But that wasn't what spoke to me that day. It was the town. It was a really run-down town on its last leg. One night, there was a gang related incident that involved one of the characters' daughter during her 15th birthday celebration, her quinceañera. The coach had previously been offered a job in Palo Alto and after that incident, he decided he was going to take it. He would move his family to an upscale town and he would teach at a private school. His daughters would attend the school and they would live well. It was his wife who didn't want to leave. They had bonded with the local Latino community and she saw the strong family ties, the strong work ethic, and how protective of the family the community was. She had grown to love the town and its people despite its state of poverty and having so little to offer.

I realized that day that it doesn't matter what a town looks like. It's the heart. Does the town have heart? Do the people have a strong sense of community? It is usually the smaller towns that form close bonds and watch out for each other. Those beautiful, expensive neighborhoods aren't always the warmest or most generous in human spirit.

And that is how we wound up in this small, dusty town. And along with the dusty town we have good neighbors who look out for one another. There are the ugly parts and then there are the charming parts. But there is community here and once people in this town get to know you, they take care of you during hard times.

This house was dingy and filled with depressing energy. We worked on it for an entire month before we moved in. I would visit and unload a truckful of garden goods and supplies in the backyard while Bali and our handyman worked on the house. I would take a tour, but after walking through it, I would go home feeling heavy and blue. It was as if I'd absorbed all the years of dark energy that had filled the house for years. Drug addiction, poverty, homelessness, mental illness, prostitution . . . they had all resided in those rooms and left behind their gray residue.

I did feel called to the town, though. It felt quiet and much smaller and slower than the city I was leaving. There was a quiet freeway to the new town instead of the ten-lane highways and interstates that I had to drive on just to get to parks and stores where we lived at the time. I would drive out here, passing acres of orchards and alfalfa fields instead of the busy industrial areas and suburbias I was used to.

I decided to give the new town a chance, and I must say that it has grown on me. Real love takes time and work, and this is true not just for relationships, but for cities, towns, and sad little houses that become homes.

This house went from an ugly, sad little stucco to a sanctuary for all of us. But it took a lot of scrubbing, good music, open windows, and healing energy to get it right. The town has taken some getting used to. We've had to learn to accept things the way they are, to let go of our longing for it to be this way or that way, and most importantly, to be fine with it all.

The people here are good, solid people. They have been through hard times and poor times. Farming is hard work and often doesn't pay enough. The town was also hit by a methamphetamine epidemic brought on by a group of Hells Angels in the '70s that destroyed many families and almost destroyed the community. It's taken around 40 years for it to recover, but lately, the old downtown has been revived. Old houses like mine are being purchased and fixed up. They are rebuilding roads and bridges, planting lots of trees on main streets, tearing down old, ugly shops, and building nice ones to replace the gray lots. I love that instead of sprawling out and building elsewhere, leaving the old town to be neglected and fall apart, they are revitalizing and rebuilding right in the old parts; the ugly parts, and making them lovely again. The town is doing a great job.

There are many older, tree-lined streets. We like to walk down the nicer streets and parts. I love certain sections, and when I'm out walking with Molly and the boys under huge, old trees, or out in my front garden and I lean on the fence to chat up a neighbor, I feel like I could live here forever.

Then I see the police across the street for the fifth time this month, or stumble down an alleyway with trash everywhere, or go into our local Dollar Tree and see all the filth and things strewn on the floors, and I'm ready to pack up and leave.

It angers me, because keeping your home or store clean and neat, and having pride of ownership and being grateful to even have shelter in these times should be a given. A shop owner or manager should take pride in their store and be grateful for the work and paycheck. Unfortunately, some people lack work ethic, while others are polluted with drugs.

When we first moved here, I found a mountain town about 35 miles up the way and fell in love. I was trying to find hiking trails and wound up at the ranger station. They handed me a map, obviously not knowing the lady they were dealing with. I don't even know west from east until the sun rises or sets.

I found a trail with an address on my phone and headed in that direction, the Garmin GPS leading the way. We wound up at an outdoor forest Earth school for kids of all ages. I had no idea that it was a school when we stumbled upon it that day. I walked past a big bench in the form of a dragon made from clay and straw. I continued up the path and came across a group of children and adults. They were laughing while they did various activities. There was a pond edged with cattails and a large yurt all nestled in the forest. I spotted children leaping off a tiny dock, adults standing about in groups. I also saw strange things such as deer hides on the ground and mortar and pestles with acorns mid-grind, and dream catchers hanging from oak tree branches. I didn't know what to think, so I assumed it was some strange family reunion at this forest park and trail.

I approached a man and asked if they were having this family reunion and he explained that it was a summer camp for kids. This was an Earth school. He pointed to the public trail. I took the boys and we enjoyed a nice walk through the woods, but I was more than interested in this school. When we returned home, I found it on the Internet. I also found a TED Talks video of a young kid who was sharing his experience with homeschooling and how much he was thriving, and this outdoor forest Earth school was a part of it. I signed Arjan up for a full year that night.

Arjan is my eldest son. He's been going to the school on and off; this will be his third year. Sam started last year. It's the best thing ever. I can't begin praising this school enough. It mixes Native American practices with learning to navigate, survive, and appreciate our planet. Children start as young as age four and continue into their teen years, and then they volunteer. They grow up in this forest.

In this day and age, children are growing up surrounded by so much technology and social media, the stresses of public schools, peer pressure, and the fast pace. At this forest school, they learn to slow down and be quiet; to live without cell phones, build community, find their tribe, find a love of Mother Earth, and even survive in the wilderness. There are no iPads here. I've never seen a teenager with a cell phone in his hand. They are learning what we took for granted as kids, growing up with pay phones and home phones still attached to the wall. We played and talked because there were no distractions in the '70s and '80s.

When my sons grow up and perhaps join the rat race and have big stressful jobs and lives, they will know where to go to find peace and calm, to reconnect with nature. One day when Arjan or Sam call me and say, "I'm freaking out, Mom!" I'll say, "Go to the forest, Son!"

I have since created a community with the parents and teachers as well as the town. I am a co-op member of the local health food store, and I spend hours in their library, writing and enjoying the beautiful forest view through the huge glass window. I meet strangers and share deep conversations that end in hugs and blessings. It is home to me. We keep searching for that other cottage and land up there in the mountains, and one day it will happen.

In the meantime, I stand here and wash dishes, gazing through my kitchen window at all my little brown finches who gather on the camellias. I want to take this house and my little birds with me, but I can't. More than likely we will keep the house and rent it out. It's an investment. That is what we say, but the truth is that Bali and I have a deep heart connection to this home that has served us so well for over two years and we just can't give it away. It is family now.

Chapter 3

The Healing Effects of Family

This morning, I read Sammy a stack of books that I borrowed from the library. The first one was *The Scarecrow* by Beth Ferry. A real tearjerker. It's the sweet rhyming type of tale I enjoy. The story is about a scarecrow who's out in a field all alone, season after season, doing his job of scaring away animals, because that is all he knows. One day, a baby crow falls from a tree and is injured. The scarecrow does something out of character and breaks his pole to bend down and scoop it up and tend to it. The baby crow heals and grows in the scarecrow's heart of straw and they become unlikely friends. The crow flies off when he is grown, and the scarecrow is alone. Unfortunately, he now knows what it feels like to have companionship and he is broken-hearted. With his broken pole and broken heart, he sags in the fields, enduring the seasons. Ah, but spring comes, and the crow returns and fixes the scarecrow right up, mending his pole and adding more straw. He brings with him a mate and they build a nest in the scarecrow's chest, where his heart would be, and then there are baby crows. In the end, all the animals are gathered around the scarecrow and he will be alone no more. I wept reading this story.

I weep even now because I was very alone for 40 years of my life. I had some family, and I always had friends, but there is nothing like having your own family; your own children to fill you up in the most real and nourishing way.

Before I got married and had children, I was on a huge quest to heal from a very unhappy and abusive childhood. I studied Wayne Dyer, Iyanla Vanzant, Deepak Chopra, and a lot of Louise Hay. But it was during my time taking classes through the Center for Spiritual Living that I really found healing and change.

I learned that I could change my life through new thoughts and making wise choices daily in order to redirect myself into a better future, that if I healed my mind and changed my thoughts and feelings, I would transform myself and my life.

I also quit all my bad habits. I was a nighttime smoker who enjoyed smoking pot and drinking beer far too often. I was getting nowhere with those habits. I did everything to overcome the habits and to change my life. And with commitment, hard work, and devotion, it worked. By the time I was 39 I had a very good life. I had a good job, a hound dog, two mean cats, and I lived in a pink Victorian house by the sea.

But it was when I got married, had my first baby, and became a housewife that I felt truly safe and happy for the first time in my life. That's not to say that I didn't struggle with other things. There was still my addiction to the news and the abominable Facebook. Once those were eliminated, I entered a new level of peace.

For the first time in my life I was being taken care of. My husband works hard, and he works any job he must in order to provide for us. He never complains, never states whether or not he likes a certain job or boss, never entertains unhappiness. Work is a way to feed and shelter his family and he is grateful for it. He takes pride in whatever job he does, be it managing a gas station or being a cashier earning $10 per hour.

I have never been taken care of in all my years. I took care of my mother from a young age, as she was a mentally unstable alcoholic. I then went on to struggle and take care of others who had issues as well, because that was comfortable; it's all I knew. I am a fixer and caretaker at heart, but not so much now, except for when it comes to my little family.

Bali changed that. He cleaned house, so to speak, of the last of my friends who he felt had too many issues. In his broken English, he lovingly said to me, "If you want a good life, then you can't surround yourself with lower level people." He had a normal childhood in Punjab, India. But it wasn't without troubles. He lost his father early, his brother passed away before he came along, and his sister had an autoimmune disease. It wasn't easy, but they were taken care of financially, lived in a small village surrounded by good neighbors, family, and community. He had a natural and loving childhood. He is not used to dysfunction or addiction. He doesn't allow it in our lives at all.

One evening, before we were married, he said he could see that I had been hurt by someone (I hadn't shared my past with him yet) and he wanted to be the one to heal that pain. Over the past eight years, he has done just that with his kindness and patience. He gives me space to spin in circles and gently guides me back to the safe place of our home. Sometimes he gets upset at my manic worries and is quite blunt about it, but bickering is as serious as it gets between us.

If I bring a "strange" character home, he will be polite, but as soon as they leave, he will let me know that it's best they don't visit again. They are usually troubled and were trying to find a kind heart to pull on. Once you have children you can't afford to have people like that in your life. Now that I'm a mother, I'm intensely picky about who comes into our home, our lives, and what sort of people surround my children and family. I only select those who are positive, sane (we are living in modern times, after all), and have good energy.

People have issues, but there is a difference between dealing with an elderly parent or a special needs child and just living in a state of self-created problems.

I often think back to something I read in *Becoming a Better You* by Joel Osteen, "It doesn't matter how great the potential in the seed, if you don't put it in good soil, it will not take root and grow."

The people we surround ourselves with is crucially important. Bali understood this. I was used to dysfunction. If Bali hadn't done some housecleaning and kept up on it, I would still be wasting time with people who would drag me down.

Today, I have a nice writing career and a delightful YouTube channel. We have created a cozy, safe, nurturing home and all of us are thriving. I'm happy to live a life that includes just children, a husband, and dogs. I don't feel the need to have all these friends calling me, visiting and distracting me from my work of mothering, homeschooling, homemaking, cooking, writing, and gardening. Because of that, we have slowly drawn good people into our lives over time. I have a few very close friends – a couple of girlfriends from my childhood that have made the long journey with me – and we are finding our true tribe.

My children have given me the most healing. I give them unconditional love and they give me a love in return that I've never before experienced. It is deep; a devotion that transcends time. The bond that I have with my sons will last lifetimes.

Since the boys were born, I have held them in my arms and nursed them at my bosom for years. In America, mothers are encouraged to stop nursing after a year. Many women have wisely ignored this and continue for a couple of years, but in other countries a child might be nursed up to age five. It's said that a truly healthy and well-balanced child needs at least three years. I nursed my first son for over two years and the youngest was fortunate to get over four years of bonding from nursing. He would have nursed until high school had he gotten his way.

I had to ignore many looks and comments from family. I nursed far beyond what others felt was appropriate and I had my children sleep in my bed. All very un-American behavior, but my husband agreed, as he comes from a culture that places the child and family first. Children nurse for as long as they want to; they share the family bed and they are coddled for years. They are also very bonded and devoted to their parents, often staying with them when they are grown, and bringing their wives and families to all live together under one roof. This might sound like a nightmare to some, but the love is good and strong like that with some families.

Because of the years of nursing and holding my boys from the minute they came from my body, because I never returned to work, and I've even chosen to homeschool, my sons and I are very close.

My boys are welcome to go to public school if they'd like, and Arjan did try it out for a few months. He liked many aspects of it, but was bullied daily and relentlessly. He was brave about it and didn't complain, but I knew something was happening at school that was wearing on his tiny soul, and once we talked about it, we worked with the school to put an end to this cruelty. It didn't end, and he never mentioned it again for fear of appearing weak. I knew it was still happening because I know my boy. I pulled him out the next day after a heart to heart talk.

Both boys are now enrolled in an independent study program with a wonderful charter school in our favorite mountain town. Once a week they have a full day of enrichment classes, running wild at the outdoor forest school.

I had no idea how to homeschool. I started reading all sorts of accounts and personal stories about how and why people choose to homeschool and how well it worked out for them. I studied many of the home educating styles and methods – and there are a lot! I read about Waldorf, Montessori, Classical, Thomas

Jefferson, Unschooling, Free Range, and Traditional, to name a few. I was also fascinated with New Finland and how they transformed their school system over 40 years ago. It used to be like our Prussian education system, but it was failing miserably, as is ours today. So, they did an overhaul and presently, they are recognized as having top notch schools, low dropout rates, and students who have top scores in all national testing. Not only that, but the students are happy and thriving, and teachers enjoy their careers. Why? What are they doing?

First off, children enjoy a full and long childhood. Children not being allowed to have proper childhoods today is heartbreaking. Childhood lasts for such a short time and it is a magical time of learning through play, discovery, and friendships. With the New Finland style and the Waldorf style, children spend two years in a preschool playing outdoors, baking, listening to fairy tales and learning through song, music, and unstructured play. Their childhood is fun, cozy, and nurturing of their spirits. They learn about themselves, their feelings, friendship, and community. It's not until they are seven years old that they begin to learn math and reading, and it is done in a way that incorporates art and music. They learn a second language as well as other skills such as woodworking, gardening, and knitting.

The days are only four or five hours long, there are many long breaks to play outdoors, and *no* homework, *ever*. The teachers don't spend hours after work grading papers. They spend time with their families. Children go home and play some more and enjoy their parents and siblings.

And what kind of community is created from this style of schooling? How do the children turn out? They turn out happy, smart, confident, and healthy.

With our grim public school system, the dropout rate was something like 60% at one point. I heard it on one of those big news stations years ago. The suicide rate for kids under 15 years old has quadrupled since the '80s, and I just heard on the radio news station that it's increased by 17% in the last few years.

It's the same reason 70% to 80% of adults are addicted to something, be it drugs, pills, pot, liquor, gambling, shopping, or sex, among many other things. It is stress and an emptiness inside that can't be filled with addictions and vices.

I don't want this for my boys, but I can't afford the fantastic Waldorf schools.

So, being a queen of the budget and clever at finding the less expensive path, I created my own Waldorf/New Finland style at home. I mixed in some unschooling and free range and voilà! We now have happy, healthy, super smart boys. It took a couple of years and I'm still figuring it all out. The unschooling part is new to us. I had been fighting with my eldest over math, to the point of yelling. A few souls suggested that I investigate that method and I took that seriously. Spirit sends important messages through others, you know.

One book that really helped to change my perspective was *Free to Learn* by Peter Gray. It really opened my eyes to the idea of letting my children find their way of learning through play and freedom.

It feels so good to have my children here with me. I'm writing in my pajamas this Sunday morning, listening to good music. Arjan is working on his art. He draws and sketches all day; it's his passion and he can dive deep into his love of art all day if he so chooses. He is also an avid reader. We have two huge bags that we take to the library to fill with fresh stacks of books, then haul back when we return them. He and I could read, sketch, and write all day. Sam doesn't know how to read yet and he was very resentful that we taught Arjan to read. He blames that skill for the loss of a companion.

Sam loves to play in the garden and cook. We bake and try new recipes all the time. When I work in the garden, he keeps me company as he plays Godzilla among the eggplants, building cities with empty flower pots.

Dad takes the big dogs to the river to run, but the boys and I take our little Molly for walks in the neighborhood, showing off all her 18 inches of cuteness. The high school girls love her. They "ooh" and "ahh" over her as she wiggles past them on her tiny legs.

I'm not much of a dog person despite the fact that I have three at home. For years, I asked the Universe to not send any more. My big boys are good dogs and I love them so. Clyde is my hound and first furry son. He is stubborn and doesn't mind at all. He acts inappropriately when guests arrive, giving them a hard time. He drags me down the street when I walk him, and he chases or barks at everything. But he is our protector, mighty and fierce about his family. Babu is smart and does everything to please. He is frightened by his own reflection in the windows at night, and I don't know that he would fare well against a burglar. I would have to protect him. I love Babu for his weakness and humble ways and we cuddle and kiss every morning. Clyde is handsome and smart and hard to love on as he wiggles and jumps too much. Whenever he pees on my lettuce or poops in my garden beds, I count down his years of life on Earth as I watch him from my kitchen door. We have put up a fence around my main garden because of these habits.

Then Molly came along. I thought I wasn't a small dog person. I thought Dachshunds were the most bizarre-looking dogs. Really, what happened with the genetic makeup? Long bodies, tiny legs, pointy snouts. But she was handed to me by neighbors who said that she was too much for them. I looked down at my bundle, wondering if I would bond with her, as I carried the pup across the street to my yard and a very displeased husband.

She is the love of my doggie world! I have never loved a dog or cat like I love her. She is so delicious and fun, so smart, and almost human-like. She sleeps at my feet when I wash dishes. She follows me everywhere, never letting me more than a few feet out of her sight. She whines and tries to climb into my lap when I write at the table and is a devout cat chaser. I use her to break up cat tiffs on my front porch, even though I know that she can't catch them. They always return, as I do like to feed the strays. I just don't enjoy the occasional cat spat.

The boys and I adore her so much that when we don't have her with us, we talk about all the ways that we are charmed by her. I always get a shrill and yappy lecture from her when I return home. She detests me leaving her, even for five minutes. I am forever a small Dachshund devotee.

With Arjan and Sam, I have learned that if you create an environment that is filled with learning tools and opportunities, the children will direct themselves. We have PBS KIDS and ABCMouse for our media. Arjan loves documentaries about our planet, other countries, animals, and dinosaurs. Since we take weekly library trips, he has his own card now, and he knows how to navigate the Internet and order all of the books that he's interested in. I select piles of books for Sam that are filled with wonder, with lessons on love and sharing, and all sorts of life stuff. I still read to him almost nightly. In the morning, if we start off with a few books, it puts him in a good space.

If the boys show an interest in a certain topic, I get books, movies, documentaries, and even toys to support them. No interest is ever considered silly or worthless. Sam loves Godzilla so we watch both the classic and new Godzilla movies, build cities and act scenes out, and come Christmas I will get him a Godzilla toy.

Arjan was into farming, then construction, and then dinosaurs . . . and *that* never ended. We bought toys, went to farms, watched documentaries on farming, went to construction sites, read books on all that is farming or construction (written for his age range, of course). Then we did the same with dinosaurs. We have what seems to be thousands of dinosaur toys by now. Molly has helped with the decluttering of these toys by selecting one to chew on each night. I don't fuss much about it, as I'm a bit happy to see some go, and she somehow always chooses the cheap ones. I put the valuable ones up and away from her reach.

I used to watch PBS with my little guys. They play so many wonderful programs for children. I loved watching Peg + Cat explore history and do math in fun ways. Daniel Tiger's Neighborhood was a bit whiny for me, but he teaches about friendship and feelings. I loved and still love Curious George. Wild Kratts teaches about animals all over the world, Sid the Science Kid was great, and then we had our beloved oldie, Sesame Street.

I would bring my big mug of delicious coffee into the living room and watch Sesame Street or Daniel Tiger's Neighborhood with the boys, reliving a childhood I never had. I would watch Disney movies with them. What usually ended up happening is I would really get into the movie, and the boys would get bored and go do other things. We would go to three different parks almost daily and I would climb, slide, and run with them. Mostly I was afraid to let them run around and explore so high up, so I joined them, but I got some exercise and relearned to play. At home, I would help Arjan build cities with all the toys we had purchased from thrift stores or that friends had given us since their children had outgrown them. We had airports, train tracks, cities, and dinosaur parks. I loved building these elaborate towns throughout our tiny 800 sq. ft. rented house in Sacramento.

Today, our house is also filled with art supplies and books. They can learn to garden, cook, shop, and clean with me. There is a lesson in everything, but the biggest lesson for them is that this home is a sanctuary. Buddhists live in temples on mountains their whole lives. They occasionally venture out to the city now and then to pray for others, guide groups in meditation, or perhaps to receive donations. But they live peacefully in their sanctuaries.

I've created this home with love and lots of color. I've filled my home with bright patterns and plants, and my yard with fruits, nuts, and gardens. I've built bird baths, homes, and feeders and plant flowers for the bees. My yard is so thick with birds during the spring, it's a birdwatcher's dream. During the rest of the year it's a finch's haven. I see them in my camellia tree outside my kitchen window. They have a big community in that one tree alone.

Since I feed the stray cats well, they leave my birds alone, and I haven't seen one mouse or rat inside or outside of my house. With all the food we have growing, I should have a community of those as well, but the cats take care of that. My neighbor says she is rodent free as well, and no longer looks at me crossly when I fill the bowl on my porch with cat chow.

I love my life more than I ever thought possible. We are not rich. We don't travel to Europe or take trips to Disneyland. We drive old cars and live in a little house that is getting fuller all the time. But we are happy, truly happy.

We do go out often, but there are days that string together and the only time we have left the house was to walk Molly. Our home offers everything to fill the soul, to explore interests, to keep us busy playing, creating, and pondering.

A good family can fill you all the way up, giving you a life that is fulfilling and at the very least, pleasant; but one must grasp it with the whole heart and both hands. Settle into this life and appreciate the love that a good mate and happy children fill a home with.

At times, I find that I can be too militant and try to be structured because I'm afraid the boys will fail, or that I will be judged as not being a good mother. But when I stop trying to impress others, when I don't give one hoot what others are doing or thinking, and when my top priority is my family's happiness, that is when it all comes together. It is then that we thrive.

Motherhood and homemaking should never be a competition. It should be playful, nurturing, and filled with love and patience. I don't have these qualities all at once at all times, but I try my best. Ever since I read *Parenting With Love and Logic* by Foster Cline and Jim Fay, I am able to observe other parents and I recognize the beautiful and soft ways toward their children. I also observe the parents and wives who aren't so lovely, be it in real life or in movies, and make mental notes of what NOT to do or how NOT to behave. Although we shouldn't compare ourselves to others, we can still learn from their behavior so that we can become aware of who we do or don't want to become.

I work on myself constantly. I grow. I heal old wounds. I feed myself and fill myself up with spiritual food constantly. I analyze my behavior after all sorts of situations where I came up short, and I think about how I would do things differently if I had a second chance. And I always do get a second chance.

My children pick up on everything having to do with me. I can smile and act as if all is well; but if I'm upset, my children feel it, and it agitates their little souls. It is my duty and priority to keep myself sane and happy, to be grounded and mentally healthy for them.

An unhappy, naggy wife and mother makes her husband sour and her children sick. So, along with a clean and charming home, nourishing and tasty cooking, clean clothes, and smart management of the household money, a mother and wife needs to find her happiness.

It is not selfish; it is crucial for the survival of the house and family.

With my husband's patience for his wife's growth and healing, and my children's deep love and devotion for their mother, I have found great happiness. I have also followed my heart in discovering my hidden talents and encouraging them. My writing and YouTube channel are such a fun, creative outlet. I just have to be mindful not to put any of those projects before my family and home duties.

I also find that eating extremely healthily and attempting to exercise daily keeps me balanced and well at heart. I love my coffee drinks, so I have everything at home to make amazing drinks in my kitchen. I love sweets and bake cakes and such, but I try to not overdo the sugar. We tend to eat mostly vegetarian and plant-based. We consume plenty of fruit, vegetables, grains, and beans. We take vitamins. We go outside for the sun and fresh air and to move our bodies.

Although I often don't get as much exercise as I'd like, and I eat more sweets that I should, I wake up every day and schedule in some physical activity for us and sauté a pan of vegetables. It's for health and not vanity.

The key to my overall happiness has been living a wholesome life free of addictions (besides espressos and cake), finding a hobby I can throw my whole self into at times, and letting my family find what they love as well.

Chapter 4

My Personal Grocery Store and Café

My kitchen and pantry are my happy and creative places in our home. The dining room table also turns into a creative and happy place when I sit and write my books or blogs. I put the leaf in the table to make it large enough to accommodate all of our daily writing and drawing projects. I used to reserve the leaf just for dinner parties or holiday feasts, but lately we all seem so busy at the table with different projects.

But the kitchen is where I make all sorts of delicious, hot meals and bake soft, chewy breads to slather butter on. It's where I spend much of my time.

I have been working on our diet for years, finding ways to fit more and more vegetables in and create a diet loaded with goodness and nourishment. Right now, we eat almost all organic and about 90% plant-based. I will never be one to become rigid or hardcore with our eating. I just want the foods we eat to be clean and packed with nutrition, so that we thrive in health. Health is one of the keys to happiness. Mental well-being and spiritual strength are also essential, but food is big. We love trying new dishes. It feels so good to have a delicious meal waiting for you, that you can't wait to dive in with your fork.

We became vegan one year. That was the most fun I ever had learning new dishes, because I had to veganize all of our favorites. I loved watching cooking videos on YouTube and learned so much about seasoning. However, I still need a video or recipe to follow. As much as I love to cook and eat, it isn't second nature when it comes to working with herb combinations.

We went back to meat after a year. I can't remember why. I think I started being too strict and listened to everyone's advice on cutting this and that out. "Follow the McDougall Program." "Cut out salt and oil." "Don't use alternatives." Blah, blah, blah. I seem to have lost the fun aspect and then the cravings started. I really do like meat. And cheese. And grass-fed milk. I just don't like how animals are treated and I feel and look so much better, younger, and healthier when I cut it all out. I love having a compassionate diet. My conscience is clear.

We recently went back to a plant-based way of eating, and I've taken it to a whole new level. First off, vegan alternatives have grown in number and variety. The vegan movement has exploded and spread all over and now I can get vegan butter, milks, cheeses, sausages, and so much more anywhere! Even big box stores or stores that wouldn't even humor plant milks a year ago have special sections for the plant-based chef: Walmart, Target, Raley's Supermarkets, even local markets.

I was also introduced to a book and a documentary that would change the way we eat in a big way.

We had traveled to Oregon to meet some folks and check out their off-grid homestead. The woman told me about *The New Farm Cookbook* by Louise Hagler and how she makes her own gluten to make wheat meat. I ordered the book the minute we returned home, and I absolutely love it. It takes me to a very hippy, natural, happy place. I've transformed my kitchen and learned to make my own soy milk along with the gluten for faux meats.

Then we watched the documentary *The Game Changers*. That was the last push I needed to return to a vegetarian diet.

My kitchen has been bustling with washing starch out of globs of wheat, boiling soy milk, and jars of sprouts growing in my kitchen window. I have restocked my pantry with organics and buckets of bulk ingredients to do all my scratch cooking.

Surprisingly, despite all the organic food I've been purchasing, my grocery budget has shrunk considerably. Part of the reason is because I've stocked up on bulk ingredients and ordered through a co-op at a discount, but also because when you cook from scratch and there are no pre-packaged convenience foods, especially no junk or store-bought snacks, you save a huge pile o' money.

One morning, while blending soybeans and baking potatoes, I was listening to Dr. Joe Dispenza. He was telling the story about how his daughter, a great manifester, had decided that she wanted a shopping spree. To make a long story very short, she did it, and not with her father's help. She and her friend were blessed with a huge shopping spree compliments of an old client of her friend's father. I was listening and taking mental notes and I thought, "I would *love* a shopping spree!" But I have everything. My house is fully decorated, our wardrobes are large and complete. I have everything I need and want. However, I had just jumped into the new way of cooking and my pantry was barren at that time. We were on such a strict budget and I was waiting for payday to do a little shopping. I thought about how I would love for someone to just offer me a big chunk of money and tell me it was only to be used to stock my pantry. Two days later (maybe even less than that), a wonderful lady who has been a big blessing in my life emailed me. She said that she had been watching my recent videos and wanted to send me money to stock my pantry! Not only that, it was exactly the amount I was desiring!

When the money came a couple of days later, I needed a few days to just absorb the abundant gift. I sat and carefully planned out how I would spend every penny of this gift to the fullest. This is when I learned that shopping in bulk with the co-op was a big money saver. Making faux meats from flour is a new concept but it makes some pretty tasty things and saves so much money. Then there is the soy milk. Homemade is different from store-bought, that is for sure. You must work with it a bit. Add some salt, vanilla, cook some dates in the batch, add more sweetener after it's cooled . . . I'm still working on it, but let me say that it costs me $1.50 or less to make a gallon of soy milk and it costs $2.99 to $3.99 to purchase a half gallon at the store.

I don't miss working with meat. My kitchen smells fresh and herbally now. It smells like fresh bread cooling and tomato sauce simmering. Occasionally, I do cook up a big pot of bone broth for the dogs. It's good for them in their senior years. I don't enjoy how my kitchen smells then.

I have no pantry, really. I've converted my laundry room and water heater closet into my pantry. The laundry room is very airy and cool, so I don't have to worry about steam. It has a back door and a big window, and the kitchen and one of the bedrooms are off this pantry/laundry room. We bought some kitchen shelving units and put one in the water heater closet, found another small one on the street and put that under the window. With my pantry money gift, I filled our 5-gallon buckets with baking flour, wheat flour, steel cut oats, and brown rice. I stacked the shelves with mixes, nuts, coffee beans, and lentils. These foods add perfectly to my previous supply of walnuts, black beans, and oats.

WinCo Foods is great for buying in bulk on a tight budget. A large family could easily stock up well with only a few hundred dollars at this store. But we are going organic. That isn't possible for everyone, and I know this. If one really needs to stretch the dollar, WinCo Foods and Grocery Outlet are the go-to places. I also find lots of organics and vegetarian items at Grocery Outlet at a great price.

Back when we had a big money-saving goal and I wasn't as intense with the organics, I could take $300 to WinCo Foods and stock up on enough food for a month's worth of menus. This would also fill the pantry with items that would stretch for a couple of months when combined with what we already had stocked.

At Grocery Outlet, I buy cheap bubble bath and huge bottles of shampoo and conditioner that last a year or more. They have big packs of 12 bars of Dove and Irish

Spring soap (the only soap that is considered manly enough for Bali). I can also buy mascara for one dollar, tinted face creams for a few dollars, and Revlon hair dye for a couple of bucks. At other stores, tinted face creams are more than $10 each now, and Revlon or L'Oréal hair dye can be around $6 or more per box.

I also use my bank card often to earn points. Now and then I get a $25 Target card and can really stock up on our toiletries.

Coffee is a big deal in my life. I have let go of many vices, but coffee will remain until the end of this lifetime. I used to have a Mr. Coffee drip coffee maker. He was fine, but broke down one day, and that was not fine.

Around the same time, I had been reading blogs about old-fashioned homemaking. I'd also read the delightful book *Made from Scratch: Discovering the Pleasures of a Handmade Life* by Jenna Woginrich. I had begun to buy things that didn't need plugging in. A hand-crafted broom had recently joined the family, and after Mr. Coffee passed on, I ordered a stovetop percolator. After watching the movie *Eat Pray Love,* I added an Italian stovetop espresso maker and later, after a visit with a friend, I added a handheld milk frother that that really rocked my coffee world. Now I make homemade lattes, mochas, Americanos, and cappuccinos. Sometimes I simply go for an oversized mug of creamy, frothy, milky, sweet coffee to start my day the right way.

I would never become an instant coffee drinker or buy a Keurig Coffee Maker. I set the percolator or espresso pot on the stove and jump into a hot, bubbly shower. When I get out, as I lather on the lotion, I can smell the brewing coffee wafting through the house. That, to me, is luxurious living.

I don't know if I can put into words what a fully stocked pantry does for the kitchen goddess' soul. To have an abundance of spices, herbs, sauces, mixes, and sugars. To have big glass jars filled with trail mixes, dried fruits, nuts, brans, odd ingredients like powdered cheese, powdered peanut butter, nutritional yeast, oils, and seeds. To have big 5-gallon buckets filled with all sorts of grains and flours and beans.

I can whip up a meal or a cake, a casserole or loaf of Amish bread anytime, any day. I just shop my pantry, pull out the ingredients, and get busy in my kitchen.

And just like a café owner, you must rotate and take inventory every now and then. I have an ongoing list of items that I need, and when it gets long enough, I head up the mountain to my favorite health food store and put in a big order. Then, while I'm there, I do a bit of shopping from the bulk bins for smaller amounts of herbs and perhaps some coconut sugar.

As one of my subscribers put it, "Stocking my pantry has become a hobby." I love finding deals and when I have extra funds, I feel like I'm going clothes shopping as I drive off to WinCo Foods to load up my cart. I fill my pantry and kitchen shelves with scratch (and sometimes not so scratch) goods. After all, do I *always* cook from scratch, and do I *always* have the energy or time? No and no. There are times that we are running around, and I must whip up something fast before someone's sugar drops and a fit ensues. Or I'm in the middle of a huge writing project and it's just easier to shove a giant Stouffer's frozen lasagna into the oven and let it cook itself.

Many really accomplished homestead wives or mothers of large broods are far more practical than I am. They cook large batches of food ahead of time. They double recipes when they cook and then freeze extra casseroles and lasagnas. They are so smart. It only happened one time for me. My excuse is that I don't have enough casserole baking dishes. I only have one glass one right now that I found at a thrift store.

I buy cake mixes when they're $0.99, and macaroni and cheese when it's $0.50 per box. I load up on cans of corn and green beans, and piles of Campbell's Mushroom Gravy. It's the only vegetarian gravy that I love, and I only like the canned stuff. Because it's hard to find in my area, I buy 10 to 15 cans every time I visit the store that carries it. I do that in the hopes that they'll think that it's a big seller and keep it in stock. You gotta support your products.

Then there is canned cranberry jelly. I love this stuff! I eat it with everything. I also love green bean casserole anytime of the year so it's imperative that we have lots of cream of mushroom. You can make all this from scratch as well, but I detest homemade cranberry jam or jelly with the actual cranberries in it. I love the stuff that comes out of the can, in the shape of the can, with no real berries to be found, thank you.

I have never made cream of mushroom. It may be divine, but when the mood hits to make something like green bean casserole or tuna casserole, you must act fast. I love casseroles because of how quick and easy they are to assemble, which is why I was a devoted fan of *Dump Dinners* by Cathy Mitchell. I waited by the door for days after I had ordered that book. When it finally arrived, I read it cover to cover. I marked a few recipes that I thought might be real winning dinners, ran off to the store with an ingredient list, stocked up on canned goods and dry pasta, and began making dump dinners and baking nightly. I should mention that I was pregnant with Sam at the time. I was also addicted to Amish fiction, and all the characters did was work hard, praise the Lord often, and eat heartily. They cooked so many amazing casseroles, pies, biscuits, and gravies!

You can't be pregnant, read that stuff, and not cook a casserole and bake brownies or pies nightly.

Having a stuffed, loaded, and stacked pantry makes me feel **so** abundant and cheerful. I know that if we need to save big money for a few months we can create menus from our own personal little store. I know that if we fall on a challenging time, we would be fine for months.

I also like it because I go through phases of enjoying being out and about, shopping, and socializing. I then go through times when I don't want to go out, or be in stores, or even talk to people. I am cozy and safe at home and I love that I don't have to leave the house if I don't want to. We don't have any delivery services around here, so I don't have any other options. Until the day comes when they are available to me, I just prepare. I prepare for antisocial times, cold winters, writing projects and challenges, and 'no-spend' months.

A kitchen garden is also a big thing for the old-fashioned homemaker. I have an assortment of books about the depression era, and my biggest inspiration in the kitchen is *We Had Everything but Money* by Deb Mulvey.

Back in the early 1900s, and especially during the Great Depression, everyone who had a yard planted a big garden. Whether you were buying a house or renting, the land was always considered, not the house itself. The house could be a shack, but if there was land, you would be able to feed your family and maybe even make some money. The wife would do what she could to make the house livable.

Nowadays the house is all the rage, isn't it? We look at the countertops and ask how many bedrooms there are. We check out the living room to see how big it is. We don't look for land or ask, "How big is the backyard?"

I can fix up any old house with some washing, painting, and my imagination. I can decorate it with throw rugs, plants, and thrifted artwork. It's the land I look at. Is it level? Does it have brown, rich soil, or red clay? How many square feet or acres is it? I'm so greedy with land now. We only have 4,162 sq. ft. for our yard, and I have stuffed it with gardens and producing trees. I want more . . . much, much more! I am addicted to planting food. Especially when I go into the health food store and see organic nectarines for $4.99 per pound. I will leave the store, head for the nursery, purchase a nectarine tree, and plant it the next day.

Growing our own organic food is an enormous money saver. It's also the cleanest, freshest food we can get. We are going out to our backyard and picking our produce for that evening's supper. It's like we have our very own produce section right outside our kitchen door.

We've had to pull some unsuccessful trees, but we have planted many more. How it will all play out when they get big, I'm not sure, but for now they don't look intimidating. We have a Mediterranean climate here and our hardiness zone is 9b, one of the best for growing everything. So far, we have almonds, apples, nectarines, lemons, mandarins, a 3-in-1 pear hybrid, pomegranates, and avocados. We even have table grapes growing over our old pergola frame. It takes years for new trees to produce but one day we will enjoy a lot of good food. We can also grow produce almost year round. That is what I love about this area the most.

Whenever I go to big box stores and push a large cart around mile-long aisles under fluorescent lighting, I feel like I'm doing something very unnatural and unsustainable. When I go to my yard and trim a basketful of eggplant and kale, it just feels right. When I go to my pantry and pull out a bucket of flour and knead my own dough and then turn it into bread, I feel good.

Sam and I love watching *Nailed It!* on Netflix. We laugh and laugh. But I seriously want to attempt a fancy layered cake for the boys' birthdays. I do all the cooking for their birthdays and put on a big feast with family.

I love Thanksgiving with friends and family and cook up a storm for that one, too. We just had a week of Thanksgiving. We usually have friends come for

Friendsgiving and then we celebrate the day of Thanksgiving with other family and friends. This year, our friend's husband took a bit of a spill down the stairs and broke a few ribs the night before our big feasting day. Fortunately, my dear friend (who is also one of my son's godmothers) came down from Oregon and stayed all week. She helped with the boys and washed dishes so I could immerse myself in cooking. We chose to have a vegetarian feast and I cooked up a substitute turkey loaf from Quorn. We also had mashed potatoes made from Yukon Gold spuds, herb and onion stuffing, green bean casserole, mushroom gravy, cranberry jelly, and homemade cheesecake with a homemade graham cracker crust. The next day, I made more mashed potatoes, sautéed green beans with corn and red onions, and cornbread stuffing that I purchased at Trader Joe's. We feasted on that filling, delicious and pretty healthy food all week.

At Christmas, it's usually just my man, my boys, and me. I make down-home food that is comforting. I bake a lot. I make homemade sugar cookies with frosting and let the boys decorate them. I also make my easy family favorite recipes such as Buckeye Balls, Puppy Chow, and Fudge. This year I may try my hand at cinnamon candy. I pass this out to everyone: our mail carriers, dentist, doctors, neighbors, and friends.

When we visit friends or family, I like to pack a bag of groceries and cook for them. We love visiting with the boys' godparents, and when we do, I truly enjoy cooking for everyone. I make chow mein, crab and cream cheese rangoons, and homemade sweet and sour sauce. Other times Bali will make curry chicken and steamed white rice. As you can probably guess, they are overjoyed when we visit.

Chapter 5

How Frugal Living Launched a Writing Career

Over four years ago, I became inspired to follow my writing dreams, and today, I enjoy a fruitful career. I always wanted to be a writer. When I was a child, I made my own little books with cut out paper and a stapler. I wrote *and* illustrated them all by myself.

I always had journals. I would fill up books with all my confused thoughts and feelings. Every few years I would burn a boxful of them. It was therapeutic. I'm happy I didn't keep them. They were filled with detailed memories of rough and painful times I'd endured. I find that it's best to write it out, then burn and move forward into a brighter future.

When I was in my twenties, I tried to write books, but I had little experience with life and my imagination was tainted by bad habits and depression. I just couldn't write more than a page. But I would strike poses in the long mirror on the wall near my desk, pretending they were photos of me on the back cover of my books. I would be a popular author one day! I desired that strongly.

Today, I have an author's page on Amazon filled with fiction and homemaking books. I'm not famous and I don't really find that as important any longer. Now that

I'm a real live writer and loving it, it doesn't really matter. I feel fulfilled, not only as a writer, but in my home life as well. I'm blessed with my beautiful, healthy boys. I have done well. My books are enjoyed and receive positive reviews 90% of the time, with lovely, nasty reviews the other 10% as a good balance. Even Stephen King has his haters, right?

I started writing after my family moved from living on a pear and cherry orchard on the river. You would think that a life on the river would inspire a Mark Twain type of reverie. Mostly, I read. Those were my big reading years. I had two babies and no car. We lived so far out that you couldn't walk anywhere but in the orchards or around the alfalfa field. We had a huge backyard and Arjan loved to play outside in the big sandbox his father had made for him. Sam, who was just a baby, nursed and slept all the time.

We would sit in our backyard under a giant hundred-year-old olive tree. I would read stacks of Amish fiction along with books about frugal living. That was when I discovered *The Complete Tightwad Gazette* by Amy Dacyczyn. It is a frugal housewife's dream. The book is thick, filled with tons of advice on how to pinch pennies in all sorts of ways. Some of it is a little bit too much for me, but it is quite inspiring, especially her personal story. There is also a section in the back with other women's success stories that I really enjoy. I still go over these stories to keep me on the frugal path.

We were adapting to a small budget as a family. Bali only made $10 per hour as a cashier. Prior to this, we had been living in Fort Bragg and he was earning a bigger salary, running a Circle K convenience store. I had worked until I was 8 months pregnant. In addition to both of our salaries, we also had a good roommate who paid rent. Now we didn't have any roommates and were surviving on one paycheck. We went from having an income of almost $6,000 per month to just $2,800 per month. Bali had to work six days and over 60 hours per week. I can't remember all the gory details at this point, but my poor husband was gone all the time.

Prior to losing all of our extra income, I had already been practicing using grocery envelopes, bulk shopping at the beginning of the month, and keeping a written budget in a ringed notebook. I didn't shop for anything else. All we spent money on was rent, utilities, gas, and groceries. We were in good shape. We were prepared for our income to be cut in half because we had zero debt and the one car we had was paid for. We also had a large savings account that we had built up when we both worked.

After reading *The Complete Tightwad Gazette* cover to cover, I began making vats of laundry soap, hanging laundry out on the old clothesline, and picking the fruit around the farm. Previous tenants had planted fruit trees decades ago. We had mandarins, lemons, and oranges in the winter. In the summer and fall there were persimmons, pears, plums, and apples. I learned about seasonal fruit. I began baking our bread. I loved the honey wheat recipe found in some of my books, but it's not the most budget-friendly due to the large amount of honey and butter it calls for. It is delicious, though.

That time in our lives was sweet and slow. I'd be out in the backyard, holding a book, my babies playing at my feet. We would hear boats on the river and occasionally see a tractor or hay machine drive by slowly. On Sundays, we would take drives to explore the farms and tiny, old towns. My days were spent cleaning, reading, enjoying my babies, and finding ways to cut costs. With Bali working so much, I wanted to find ways to use every dime wisely, maximizing every paycheck.

Because we lived in a 1,600 sq. ft. ranch house with three bedrooms and two bathrooms, it took a lot of propane to heat it up. We had a wood stove, but we found ways to get it for free from old orchards that were being cut down and replanted. If we hauled the wood ourselves, we were free to take it. We spent every spare day gathering wood. At a nearby hot tub shop, they gave away wood trimmings that were perfect for kindling and I would go and pick up boxes of them. At one point, we had stocked up enough wood to last through a couple of long, cold winters. It saved us hundreds of dollars.

We only traveled to the nearest large town once a week. This was the day that we would typically grocery shop and play a bit. Sometimes I would leave the boys with Bali. Sam was nursing, but I also supplemented with goat milk. I would leave him with bottles of it, giving him a stern look, as I never trusted anyone with my precious babies for very long. Then I would race to town, music blaring (anything that wasn't a nursery rhyme). I only had one luxury, and that was Starbucks. I would buy myself a latte flavored by the season. During the fall, it was pumpkin spice. In the winter, peppermint mocha was my choice. With my hot latte in one hand and cash envelope in the other, I would choose one store to do my weekly shopping. That was the only time that I had some time to myself. You would think that I was on a float and on my way to a cruise ship for a long vacation. I savored and cherished this time so much. That was how simple life was for us back then. A trip to the grocery store was my two hour vacation.

This was the beginning of my writing career, but I wouldn't know this until we moved to a smaller house in town.

I began researching homeschooling when Arjan was just a tot. Along with homeschooling, it seemed that downsizing and living a very simple and frugal life were all intertwined with this lifestyle.

After some convincing, Bali agreed to move to a bigger town. A few wonderful things happened then. Bali's old boss had gotten rid of his partner who had gotten them in all sorts of debt. He needed help and asked Bali if he would take a position as a cashier until he found another gas station to buy, at which time he would make him a manager again. This was fantastic as we really liked the old boss. He was a good man; very generous and easy-going.

Bali had been unhappy at his job in Walnut Grove. He never complained, but I knew he was done when he called in sick one day, something he NEVER did, even when he was sick as a dog. I encouraged him to quit. It was an unhappy store with an unhappy family, and it was wearing on him. Because we had a big savings balance and he had other funds stored away, he did quit. But within just three weeks, he had another job. That one, in a very bad part of Sacramento, turned out to be worse. So when the old boss called and offered Bali a job in Vacaville, we grabbed it and we celebrated.

There was a bit of a commute from our house to Vacaville, but the pay was better and the environment was pleasant. You learn to be grateful for the small things because they are usually everything that is truly important in the grand scheme of it all.

I found an 800 sq. ft. house in a nice neighborhood a few miles from Sacramento. We were going from a 1,600 sq. ft. house with huge yards that required weekly mowing to a tiny 800 sq. ft. house with two bedrooms, one bathroom, and a yard the size of a postage stamp in the back. Maintenance and cleaning were reduced by 75%, leaving much more time for playing. We didn't need wood for the stove. Heating and cooling a tiny house was very inexpensive to do. Bali's commute was cut in half as we were closer to Vacaville now and with the lower rent, cheaper utilities, and gas savings, we saved over $600 per month.

The other joyful discovery was that we could walk to a big library, about three or four different parks for the boys to play in, grocery stores, and a chiropractor – the best one I have ever had. This saved tons on driving, gas, and wear and tear on the car. By then we had the truck, but I loaded the boys up in a wagon and we walked everywhere.

Bali worked a little less and was home for supper every night. We were headed in the right direction.

When we moved into this house, I sat down one morning and started writing *Queen of Penny Pinching*, my very first published book.

I had written a couple of books years ago, after my mother passed away and before I was married. It turned out that giving up my vices had the positive effect of helping me think clearly enough to write a book. One of the books was about my life with my mother from birth to what was then the present. It was a novel and so very cathartic, but I never published it. It was just part of my healing process. The next book was written after being sober for one year. I later published it under the title, *Queen of Sober*.

But this was the very beginning of working on a real-life writing career. I was so inspired! I sat in my little kitchen, at my cute second-hand table I had purchased on Craigslist for pennies on the dollar. I would watch the sun rise through the huge sequoia in the yard outside my window. I adored my new little rental and now I had time to write. I was filled with ideas, inspired by the two years spent on the fruit farm, as well as everything I had researched and practiced over the years. I wanted to share my experiences and encourage others to choose an easier way to live.

I was meeting mothers at parks who expressed a longing to stay home but felt that they couldn't. I would ask, "Why can't you?" They went on to explain that they had a five bedroom house, a leased car and minivan, and piles of credit card debt to pay for. They had a lifestyle to keep up with and it required the income from two careers. Sadly, they would have only two children and they didn't even need that leased minivan or the five bedrooms. They had made the choice to live far beyond their means and had to hire gardeners and nannies to help keep it all up. This wasn't everyone's story, but I heard quite a few very similar ones. We were in Sacramento, after all. Modern families are trying to live an image, keep up a reputation. They feel like they need a big house in suburbia, a large van for the future soccer team, and big careers with fancy titles.

But they were missing out on a real life. They life they live, the image they are trying to keep up is actually running them. The house is empty most of the week, the car guzzles gallons of gas. The housekeeper enjoys the house more than they do and the gardener is the only one enjoying their yard. The nanny is raising their children. She is the real mother. What a sad, sad life.

When the kids grow up, there is no real bond or connection. They remember the nanny fondly, but the parents were there to hand out money and pay for college; to buy the new car that they can wreck one night after partying too hard with their high school buddies.

The house is lonely and empty. The dog is lonely and bored. The yard is minding its own business, looking forward to the weekly mowing by the gardening crew.

The marriage is cold and the husband and wife are disconnected. There is no warmth or depth. Of course, I'm dramatizing and assuming most of this, although I'm sure much of it is a reality for many people trying to live this lifestyle.

Where did all the energy go? To the corporation, to the company. That was where all the extra hours, the late nights, and weekends went. Good for that company. They wisely sucked up your life and soul and got rich, rich, rich. You now have nothing of meaning, but perhaps a retirement fund you may or may not use wisely. You may be divorced and sickly from all the years of stress by the time you retire, and end up spending it in doctors' offices or sitting in your big house alone.

No, thank you. I'd rather live in a humble shack and learn to grow food to feed my family. I wanted to nurse my babies for years and watch Sesame Street with them. I wanted to enjoy my coffee in the mornings. I waited and cried, prayed, tore at my ribs and gnashed my teeth, as they say in the Bible, to have babies. It took 40 years to have them, so I sure as hell wasn't going to have someone else enjoy them.

And so, I typed and typed out all I knew. I woke at two and three in the morning to work by candlelight, brewing coffee, and watching the sun rise. Sometimes,

Arjan, wearing his little old man button up pajamas, would find me and insist that I "Get back to bed and cuddle us!" As that was one of my main duties, I wrote on my laptop on the sofa while the boys played on the floor and watched PBS. I wrote in the middle of the night while everyone snored away. I wrote and wrote and wrote.

When I was done with the book, I had a new neighbor go over it to proofread it, and then I started searching for self-publishing companies. I had no idea what I was doing, and I don't know that I ever thought I would really publish this book. Then, a company called me one day. I suppose I had filled out some form on their site. I'm so good at that, that I have solicitors calling me to this day.

It was a self-publishing company that had branched off of Hay House, a larger publishing company. They talked a good game. I was ignorant and easily wooed. I published my first book through them and lost a good $3,000 of hard-earned money that we had saved for a very long time. They did nothing, and I mean *nothing*! I had to proofread and edit my own book (not my strong point), write my biography, synopsis, and do all my own advertising. I had to design my cover and didn't have anyone to help me or go over it with. I was given a hideous website that was Pepto-Bismol pink everywhere. They took months to publish it. Then the schmucks wanted thousands more to advertise. They took 90% of my royalties, did nothing to sell the book, and promised that it would be in all the brick and mortar bookstores.

Well, I went to the local Barnes & Noble and asked about my book. I found out that it was a "print to order" book. This means that they never stock the book. It's only when someone orders the book from them that they will place a special order for that one copy.

I was a bit ticked to say the least. My husband is wise, and when I also wanted to publish *Queen of Sober*, he told me to wait and see how this all played out. After I learned that this company and their self-publishing business was a rip-off, we agreed not to invest any more money into this venture.

But I was hooked. I wanted to write more books and publish all of them. I had already begun editing *Queen of Sober* and had also started on both *Queen Housewife* and *Queen Housewife and Mama on a Budget*. What would I do now that the money purse was closed to these projects?

I did what I do best. I looked for free ways to self-publish and I ran across Kindle Direct Publishing (KDP) on Amazon. I read reviews by authors about this type of do-it-yourself publishing and one female author described it as "crazy easy." That was all it took. I could do crazy easy.

And so, for the next two years I made a hundred mistakes with this "crazy easy" program, as I didn't have a clue about Word documents or formatting, making free covers, transferring into PDF format, editing and proofreading my own books, or uploading methods for e-book or paperback editions. It was all foreign. I made every mistake and strange thing a person could do. I found myself awake at ungodly hours trying to fix a cover or get a manuscript to pass for paperback formatting. I learned SO much.

Best of all, it was all free! I published e-books on Amazon, and paperback versions using CreateSpace (now under the same roof as Amazon). My covers were handmade and free. I edited and proofread everything myself. Those last two were mistakes, but I was working with a budget of zero dollars and zero cents.

My dear husband did buy me a new laptop. It was a simple $300 laptop from Costco and it served me well for years. It might have lasted longer but it was dropped a few times and my kids got their hands on it often, shortening its lifespan. I now work on a refurbished $150 laptop that I love dearly.

I remember the wonderful feeling of earning my first $12. Then it was $40, wow!

I then dove into the world of fiction. It is another animal. It's still very hard for me to surrender to the process of make-believe and imagination.

For example, I am writing this book as a NaNoWriMo challenge. I do this challenge every year during the month of November. I've done it for the last two years and I even participate in the April and July NaNoWriMo virtual camps. I have succeeded at three of these. However, this year, I've been struggling. I tried two different fictional stories and couldn't get my mojo going until I decided to write about something I know and love: homemaking. Now I'm cruising all morning, typing at high speeds (sort of joking here) and only taking breaks to cook or chase children out into the sunny garden to play.

When I began writing fiction, I used the free covers and they were cheesy. My stories were odd and not thought out well. The grammar was terrible.

I hired a former coworker from my Living Light Culinary Institute days in Fort Bragg and she began to proofread all my books and give me input. It helped immensely. Suddenly, the reviews were less about my awful editing and more about my delightful stories. I then found that buying nice book covers boosted sales as well. As they say, "You have to spend money to make money." It definitely applies here.

But I had ways of cutting costs in these areas, too. My editor had set her own cost, but it was far less than a professional editor hired from a company, and she was an old friend which made it cozy. I found a cover designer who I loved and I still buy covers from to this day. His covers have always been nicely priced, but I found ways to further maximize my savings. He used to run promotions that allowed you to get two covers for the price of one. I would wait for a sale and double that deal as well. I can't remember exactly how I did it and James, the designer has long since discontinued this deal, probably because he got tired of me being so cheap. I used to wind up getting four covers for the price of one and stock up. Oh, how I like to stock up!

The next thing I added was a blog. My friend suggested it and I said, "Everyone and their grandmother has a blog. I will never!" Then I did, and I loved it so much. It is still active and growing but back then, it was slow to grow with only a few hundred subscribers after a year. I didn't care. It turned out to be therapeutic. It felt like someone I could talk to about all the things I loved talking about; things that would bore my friends and family. I could go on and on about cleaning and budgeting, and I just so happened to find lovely souls who wanted to hear all about it. How fun.

I tried a lot of marketing strategies using Facebook and created Twitter and Instagram accounts. I would sign up for advertisers to do what they called Facebook and Twitter "blasts." I promoted any way I could. Some of it was free, and some cost a few dollars, but I never paid over $10. None of it made a difference.

What finally made the difference was putting out money to have my books covered nicely and proofread. Then came a few good reviews by some of my readers. I began to have a handful of fans, and some are still with me today. I consider them friends. They spread the word through their social media accounts when I publish a new book.

I decided to put together a book with favorite parts of my previous books, and added some new chapters. I titled it *The Homemade Housewife*, and it took off.

When we finally made our biggest dream come true and bought this little blue home, my homemaking and budgeting skills went through the roof. I took up suburban homesteading, read backyard homestead books by the dozen, bought rescued factory chickens, hauled home a free hen coop, dug up the lawns, and planted everything I could.

I also went into overdrive with old-fashioned homemaking. I hang my laundry out a couple of seasons a year. I bake all of our bread instead of just occasionally, something I used to do to feel quaint. I cook and make foods I never imagined I would, and I even attempted to make a quilt. I do manage to sew the holes in my stretch pants and once sewed up a pillow until it was a lost cause. We are blessed with a Winco Foods as I've mentioned before, and their fantastic bulk section and I have practiced everything I've preached and almost everything I've read in all those piles of frugal living books. It all came in quite handy. And really, when you put frugality into practice, it pays off.

When it came to our home, I painted and played all the time. I have been writing books about our life here for the past two years. I also rewrote a few of my fictional books and changed their titles and covers. I was using a pen name for my fiction work, but I've now changed all the books to my name, Kate Singh so that people can find me. I've been Katherine R. Devereux and Seiji Singh, so if you see a familiar book with an author by either of those names, it's the old version. I thought that having a pen name was romantic and separated me from my homemaking books, that I would be able to let loose a bit more, to get wild! But it didn't. It just made it harder to find my work.

A couple of years ago, I discovered NaNoWriMo, a creative writing project, and I've entered it four times. I have only failed once because we had too much going on that particular month. Many people get so excited the first time that they win, but the prize is simply self-accomplishment and a paper certificate that you download off the Internet. I am always entertained by first-time winners, remembering my first time winning, too. What I do to make the pot sweeter is I buy myself a NaNoWriMo victory shirt if I finish. Sometimes I will buy a poster or a mug instead. I love having the poster on the wall and wearing my shirts around while I clean the house. It's a reminder that I'm a real live writer, for goodness' sake! I often feel like I'm no such thing, and it takes someone writing me and saying that they found my book in their local library or that they own all my books and how much they enjoy them to realize that I have succeeded. I'm not famous and the only interviews I've had were for a women's magazine called *Women's World* and *The Epoch Times*, a newspaper, but I am well-mentioned on a Facebook group that is all about *The Complete Tightwad Gazette* or something along those lines. That is good enough for me.

NaNoWriMo is good for intense training in the craft of writing a novel. It forces you to think fast and type hard. You have no time to be self-conscious or find a therapist to help you work on your self-esteem issues. You don't have time for writer's block or for your ego to sabotage the whole thing. You learn what it takes to write a novel; how complicated it is to drag a story out for 50,000 words. You feel done at around 25,000 words, and you must still find the other half of the novel. There are local groups you can join, and sometimes friends will join you, which makes it very fun and exciting, especially as you're approaching the end. When you finish, it is a feeling of pure victory and exhilaration. I feel like a true writing nerd and that is when I feel really special. That is when I feel that I have found my tribe, The Writing Nerds of the World!

I have never taken classes or courses and I may never go to writers' retreats and camps. It would be fun to meet my people, but I am also easily annoyed.

I have always had a way with writing, and I have taught myself. I did read a couple of books on the subject, including *On Writing: A Memoir of the Craft*, by Stephen King. It is a very good book, and what I got from it was that if you want to be a good writer, you need to read a lot and write a lot, constantly, and voraciously. Also, he does not plot out stories. He feels that writing an outline and developing a character kills the story before it starts. He gets an idea and then proceeds to dig out the story. I have tried it and it does work, but sometimes coming up with an outline can be very helpful. Whether you like him or not, he is a brilliant writer whose huge novels keep you turning the pages. He is a storyteller extraordinaire. Just a bit gross, creepy, and very scary at times, but brilliant. I appreciate him and have devoured a few of his books, but I must be careful which ones I choose, as some can be too disturbing.

I signed up for a year of MasterClass online, and have watched many lectures by wonderful writers including Judy Blume, author of *Are You There God? It's Me, Margaret* and *Superfudge*, Neil Gaiman, author of *American Gods* (now a series on STARZ), *Coraline*, and *Stardust*. I also watched a lecture by Judd Apatow, director of *The 40-Year-Old Virgin*, and Malcolm Gladwell, author of books such as *Blink: The Power of Thinking Without Thinking* and *The Tipping Point: How Little Things Can Make a Big Difference*.

On my shelves are a few books that I've used to inspire and figure out the path to finishing a book. Some of the titles include *How to Write a Movie in 21 Days: The Inner Movie Method* by Viki King, *Save the Cat! The Last Book on Screenwriting You'll Ever Need* by Blake Snyder, and *Romancing the Beat: Story Structure for Romance Novels* by Gwen Hayes. I like to read books on the topic of writing good movies because it helps me learn how to create a good story and create empowered heroines, passionate heroes, and dark villains. I find that watching video clips on how to build a story or movie is also helpful. I came across *Story Circle* by Dan Harmon and enjoyed it. These all teach us the craft of telling a story. I'm still working on my ability to surrender to fiction. I can write books about our lives, homemaking, and living on a small budget easily. When it comes to fiction, I still need to learn the art of taking a hero on a journey that will sweep the reader away and get them emotionally involved all the way to the end. I want the reader to feel like they don't want the story to end, or to be separated from the hero or heroine, ever. When the day comes that I write a story that my readers don't want to end, I will consider it a success.

So, I study, I listen to the great authors, I watch clips on the Story Circle and how to build characters. I watch movies, I read books of all genres and I write and write and write.

I have people ask me how I am able to write considering that I have children. The truth is, I find it very easy to fit it in. If anything, my YouTube channel takes up more time and energy. I can write early in the morning before anyone rises, or after the boys are fed a filling breakfast and are deep in play or projects of their own.

I started cooking and cleaning in mass production in order to make time for writing frenzies to finish a project. Sometimes I will spend one whole day doing all the laundry, baking multiple loaves of bread, cleaning the whole house, and making tortilla dough, chicken, and big pots of beans and rice. Then I will wake up in the morning and brew coffee, put on a little music, cook a big breakfast, and write, write, write! Later, I might take the boys to the park and let them run like mad, come back home, and set up a big lunch for everyone to fill up on. I'll wash dishes and write some more. The boys will typically go outside to play in the yard or watch some PBS for down time, then it's time for baths, eat supper, do some bedtime reading, and off to bed we all go. It's very busy, but it isn't an everyday sport. I also have months that I don't write a book at all.

If you write 1,600 words a day, you will have a novel in one month. If you are a fast typist, as I am at this point, that is just a couple of hours of work or less. So, you see, writing books does not have to be all consuming. It is only in November that it gets a little wild with the NaNoWriMo challenge, usually because I wait until half of the month is over to really get serious.

I think that if I didn't have my writing, I would become bored, lonely, and even tired of my work at home. Maybe. I'm not sure because I'm happy with being home and I used to love reading and still do. That may have been enough. But writing is my thing. I enjoy it so much. I'm like a child looking forward to Christmas morning. I can't wait to sit and write sometimes. It's a creative act and makes this life complete, colorful, and vibrant.

Chapter 6

Homesteading in Town

Homesteading in town is a different culture than real, hardcore homesteading on acreage in the country, with goats, chickens, and huge crops. It's much easier and can be somewhat of a spiritual practice or hobby. It does take some exertion and sweat, but it is also healing and relaxing. It's a way to escape in your backyard from the hustle and bustle of city living.

First off, you aren't dealing with large, wild creatures such as bears and deer. Your garden foes are squirrels and the occasional mole. Birds can be a problem but there are ways to have your birds and apples, too.

Bugs can be problematic, but I have found a sort of Zen-like thing going on in my garden. The more I let nature do its thing and I return it to some balance, the more it steps in to assist.

This year, I had a big bed of tomato plants and before I knew it, they were all thickly covered in aphids. At first I went out there with my spray bottle with a water and dish soap concoction, but then I noticed some ladybugs and decided to leave them a feast that would not be ruined by the flavor of soap. I had faith in those girls and soon, there were many ladybugs and no aphids.

Bugs munch on my greens and it used to disturb me, but now I have learned that they don't eat that much. There is plenty for all of us.

Squirrels can be detoured if you have straw with chicken poop on it. When I had hens, I used straw for their coop and then used the dirty straw on my garden beds. I never had an issue.

Snails and such can be rerouted with Diatomaceous Earth, or you can get nasty and use snail pellets.

Other than that, after a couple of years of gardening, I have found that nature just has this way of bringing balance to all situations if left to its work, without interference from poisons or chemicals.

I just received *Feeding Our Families: Memories of Hoosier Homemakers* by Eleanor Arnold. In the chapter titled "Raising and Preserving Fruits and Vegetables" the author states:

"Before large scale commercial food preserving was available, the choice between winter feast or famine for her family was made by the homemaker. It was really necessary that she plant and tend a large garden, care of which was generally her full responsibility. They would probably also have a truck patch whose care was shared between the homemaker and the male members of the family. Vegetables from these plots must be canned, dried, pickled or stored for winter usage."

In the old days, there was typically a small market in town that sold dried goods such as sugar, flour, coffee, and maybe some hardware. Grocery stores didn't show up until the early 1900s. According to www.time.com, Piggly Wiggly, the first modern supermarket was first introduced in 1916.

Families would grow as much food as possible on whatever land they had. They would plant fruit trees and forage in the woods or in fields. Today, there are too many pesticides sprayed everywhere and not much of an abundance of wild berries and greens.

Ah, but homesteading is making a comeback! I have read many books and watched many YouTube videos on the topic in the last few years. Homesteading families are everywhere, and I've heard they even have Facebook groups for apartment homesteading. Homesteading can be done at any level. Just because you aren't out milking a goat at the crack of dawn does not mean you can't claim homesteading as your hobby or occupation.

I like to think of myself as an old-fashioned mother in the making. I bake almost all of our bread weekly and cook from scratch more and more each season. However, gardening and canning is what makes me feel really accomplished.

Now, I don't see a goat or beekeeping in my future, and I can't say that I see myself making clothes at the sewing machine or knitting afghans, but you never know. I tried chickens and may do that again but those girls are more work than people know, and they stress me out. They were a bit like gangsters, and not too welcoming to newcomers.

But growing food I can do, and I'm really into it. I read backyard gardening books and watch many YouTube videos on how to plant a ton of food in a small space. I've watched the mini-documentaries about the Dervaes family on the channel *Urban Homestead* what seems like a hundred times. They have a whole farm complete with goats, ducks, and chickens, and grow enough food to feed themselves and make a profit every year. They do all this on 4,000 sq. ft., yet I cry that we don't have enough land.

I often look out my kitchen window and dream of having the garage demolished and all the cement drive and patio removed. I could do so much gardening then! Alas, my husband is not in agreement. There are so many things I would do to the backyard, but everyone claims a garage is important. I just see it as an obstacle to having a yard full of fresh vegetables. I could have a mini corn field! When we had an attached garage in one of our previous homes, we were able to drive in and enter the house that way. I found it very useful on windy, rainy days. But a detached garage in the yard is a waste of space to me. We hardly have anything in it; it's almost like we throw a piece of furniture in there every now and then to prove that it is a necessary storage space.

I enjoyed having hens, but they had issues. They were factory hens that had been rescued, so their beaks had been cut off to ensure they wouldn't peck others to death in their cramped cages. They had been vaccinated but that seemed silly since they had been so mistreated and looked like crap when I got them from Animal Place, the rescue farm. They were white, but dirty, scraggly things. I was told they would always shy away from people. One hen laid an egg on the drive over and one passed away during the night.

I found a free chicken coop on Craigslist in another town. The lady said to bring a strong person to help load it into our vehicle. She should have been honest and said, "Bring at least three WWE wrestlers to get this junky coop." It had been put together with lots of odd-sized pieces of wood, was big and heavy as ever, and Bali and I had to struggle immensely to get it out of the lady's backyard, through a narrow pathway, and to the truck. Half of it leaned off the truck all the way home.

I painted it yellow using leftover paint that we'd used in our living room. Bali put a new roof on it, and we shoved it against the fence near the side yard. We added a gate made from extra materials we had from our picket fence. The neighbor's morning glories grew over the roof. It was truly charming. So, the hens went from tiny cages in fluorescently lit warehouses to a sweet little yellow house with a full yard and a nice tree to rest under when the days were hot.

I added electrolytes and vitamins to their water and fed them good food and tons of scraps. I misted them with water and fed them frozen vegetables on sweltering days. When fall arrived, I let them roam the whole garden freely. They were in heaven. They ate leftover greens and plants and scratched for bugs all day. They became healthy and happy and ran to me whenever I appeared in the yard. I was the goddess of good food and spa-like treatment. They followed me about and pretended to listen to my thoughts. I loved hearing them cluck and coo through my open windows in warmer days. Oh, but the egg song. Holy heck, someone should have warned me about this. Whenever the girls had laid an egg, were about to lay an egg, or even thought about laying an egg, the would holler and shriek and make loud sounds that made me cringe. I would yell out the window, "Just *do* it already!"

When spring came, I wanted to spread horse manure and start my gardens, so I had to put them back in their yard. I kept the straw thick, but it got very little sun and was damp and cold in the early spring. The girls hated it and I could tell it was too damp and shady. One hen got myiasis, a hideous and disgusting infection that involves poop and maggots on the animal's rear. I bathed her and tried to treat her, but she died. It was just too late. Another hen was beginning to show signs of the infection, so I bathed her but wanted to vomit even though I was wearing double gloves. Then, a third hen that had struggled from the time I got her but seemed to have done well during the winter started to get sick again. I decided to send them to a Latina lady who had lots of land and chickens, knowing that she would know what to do with them and give them a better life. I was then left with two lovely and healthy hens, including one that Bali had rescued from his gas station.

But things got even worse. I noticed that the hens seemed lonely. Then the street hen suddenly got chick-making fever and sat on her eggs for weeks, becoming thin and baldish. I couldn't stand it anymore. I felt her pain since I had tried to make chicks of my own for over 20 years. I sent her and the other lovely hen to the Latina woman's house, and I asked her to please let the street hen have a few baby chicks before she made her into a chicken enchilada. Their new home had lots of green land to explore, a big chicken coop, a lovely barn, and a rooster!

The street hen did get to have wee ones, which made my heart sing. I later found that my hens were never really accepted by the other chickens. Eventually and very sadly, a dog got into the hen yard and ate a few of them, including my girls.

I know. This is not the happy ending you were hoping for. But I have another story. This one is a bit better, warmer, and more pleasant.

When we first moved here, there was some drama with immigration and Bali was taken from us for a while. In the meantime, I met an older woman who we later lovingly called Granny. When I lost my husband for a short period of time, I had her move in to help me with Arjan and Sam in the event that I had to run any errands. She needed a place to live and I needed a grandmother for my boys. Little did I know that she had medical issues and couldn't stay awake for more than 10 minutes. So, I had a narcoleptic elder, two boys, and no man.

I have a lot of family who are in the legal field, so I reached out for help. After they rallied to bring him home, Bali came back soon after, and everything was fine. Granny continued to live with us for a few months, until her family begged her to return home. While she lived with us, though, she was the grandmother I never had.

She was the one who encouraged me to get chickens, and when I stressed over them, she would give me a look and say, "Get over it. They're fine; they're chickens." She said it very matter-of-factly, making me feel silly for being such a nervous Nellie.

She helped me find that beastly coop and watched us load it. We had some laughs over that thing.

She motivated me to plant a winter garden and showed me how easy it was to make Amish white bread. She was the one who got me hooked on Downton Abbey. Cursed series! It was worse than drugs.

She loved homesteading as much as I did, and we would research and dream together. We cooked together and took care of one another. She loved my sons and they enjoyed having a granny for a bit. She is still very much a part of our lives and so is her family. Her grandson is a good friend of Arjan's. Sadly, they recently decided to move to Texas.

Our first garden was very lush, but it produced nothing. We got a few tomatoes and a couple of zucchini. That's right, a couple of zucchini. That is how pathetic our garden was that year.

But then I learned about Novella Carpenter. I watched a documentary about her farm in the city and I read her book *Farm City: The Education of an Urban Farmer.* That is how I learned about the magic of horse manure. I immediately found horse stables nearby and asked Bali if we should go get ourselves a load. Bali, not knowing anything about horse manure, was horrified. Perhaps he thought it was like sewage. He and I had a few rounds on this manure issue. He yelled, "The neighbors will call the city and they will come inspect our yard and take our chickens!" Silly man. I yelled back, "It's horse manure for goodness' sake!" I used stronger language than that, but I'm trying to keep the book clean. I then had to drop the subject and eventually, he came around. That's how it works with us. Once he shoveled a bit of this magic stuff, he realized how much he had overreacted. Now he can't get enough of it. We have hauled in two loads over the past two years and will be hauling another one soon.

And it *was* magic. We had an abundant crop this year. I have a huge basket filled with butternut squash and canned 16 quarts of spaghetti sauce for the winter. We ate honeydew melon for breakfast for weeks, and even now in November, we are still enjoying eggplant and zucchini goulash. I have planted plenty of greens for the winter: kale, mustard greens, and collard greens. I will use these in smoothies with all those bananas that we never seem to eat before they start to brown. I will also use them in stir fry dishes and add them to my knockoff Asian noodle soup. To make the soup, I bring a huge pot of water to a boil, then add a wonton bouillon or Pho broth mix, dry rice noodles, and an enormous pile of fresh greens from our garden. It is imperative that every leaf be washed by hand, or you will have bug soup. When I make it, we will eat it throughout the entire day. It's simple, light, healthy, and cleansing.

This morning, Arjan had some stomach issues. I took my large colander and kitchen shears, went out to our garden and harvested a huge batch of kale, mustard greens, and collard greens. I have a small section in my pantry dedicated to Asian delights. I stock up from a Korean grocery store in a neglected part of the outskirts of town. I go every six months and pick up powdered broth mixes, inexpensive rice noodles, spicy Korean ramen (you'll never go back to American ramen), and different sauces. I *love* Asian food. I am still trying to master chow mein and pad phai. I grill the wait staff at Asian Garden, but they are probably under some type of oath. All I got out of three waiters was to use canola and oyster sauce as ingredients.

I have a lot of equipment for preserving: a dehydrator, a pressure canner, water bath pot, canning tools, and stacks of jars (some unused, still in their boxes). I have plenty of storage in the form of 5-gallon buckets, 1-

gallon and half-gallon glass jars, and many jars in a variety of different sizes that I have saved from my store-bought goods. My dehydrator and most of my canning tools, pots, and jars were donated by a kind soul who was downsizing and didn't need the equipment any longer.

I've even taken to saving cans for spring. I'll poke holes in the bottoms, fill with bags of soil, and raise my seedlings in the greenhouse. This is what the old mothers did.

In *Dear Kitchen Saints*, Connie Hultquist writes, "And ya know, some of the farm mothers during the Depression era were able to feed their families well . . . they had nothing but food . . . they had their own chickens and saved their vegetable seeds from year to year and planted huge gardens . . . they started pots and containers of every kind with seedlings in the winter for spring gardens."

She goes on to talk about how they would trade eggs for sewing materials, cream from their cow for tobacco or coffee, or cash for a gallon of gas.

I love reading this stuff. It was a very simple time. Think about it. You trade some cream from your cow for a gallon of gas now and then. You didn't need much. You grew it, made it, or traded something from the farm for small supplies. Wives weren't rushing out to Dollar

Tree to load up on plastic gizmos, thingamabobs, or this and that. They weren't out driving here and there. People worked with what they had and lived at home in quiet surrender to a simple life. They were one with their land and in rhythm with the seasons. Wives worked over quilts and wood stoves while their husbands were out in the sun, working with the soil on the land. Even the children spent their days outside in the fresh air.

I know that there are parts of their lives that weren't that dreamy. It's easy to fantasize and glorify a time that we didn't suffer through. Many kids left family farms to seek out a new life in the city. They craved more. However, many children from this era write about these early times and say that if they had enough to eat, and a strong, loving family, the memories are cherished.

I have an elderly neighbor who lives two doors down from me. She remembers living with her grandmother during that time because her parents were too poor and were struggling to find work. She lived with her grandmother for about a year, until her parents were able to find work and a home for them. Her grandparents lived in a tiny town on a farm with an outhouse, and those are her most beloved memories. I love to hear her tell these stories and she loves to tell them. She loved her grandmother deeply and when I asked her what it was about her grandmother that was so special, she never specified any particular thing. What made her grandmother so special was her being there for her and being home all the time. It was all the cooking and taking care of her family. She was a busy lady and worked from sunup to sundown doing all the cleaning, washing, and cooking. Not only was she a pillar of strength, she was also the force that told the family that all is well, and will always be well.

I want to be my neighbor's grandmother. Some aspire to be famous writers or to be recognized for good works. I just want to be that mother and grandmother that my children and grandchildren will praise for generations. I want them to think of me and feel good inside. I want my boys to have thousands of good memories of a safe and loving home with Mother always there, kneading bread in the kitchen on an early morning, her coffee brewing on the stove; or out in the garden harvesting basketfuls of organic vegetables that she would later make into a delicious stir fry.

I also think about the future and how the economy loves to take nose dives now and then after an almost too prosperous time. I believe that it has some unlearned lessons that it will be learning here soon, and it may be the worst yet. I did not suffer through the last two nose dives since I had nothing either time. I lived humbly and worked simple jobs.

My husband and I are willing to work any job when times get tough. We are not too prideful to bag groceries or flip burgers. When you have a family to support, you work any job you can to earn a paycheck.

One thing that I learned from the summer that Bali was taken away for a bit, is that life is never stable. You must have a plan A and a plan B. Maybe even a plan C. I like having a few plans, really.

We have many goals, some of which we have accomplished, and others we are still working on. The first goal was to buy a cheap fixer-upper house with a mortgage (including property taxes and insurance) that was far less than any rent we had ever paid. We wanted it to be so small that if Bali ever lost his job, he could go work at Taco Bell if he had to, and we would still pay the bills with ease. We also wanted to grow as much food as possible, to learn how to cook and bake everything that we love to eat, and to preserve and can food for storage. I'm happy to say that we have accomplished all of these things.

Ultimately, we want to live small, light, and financially simple. This means no debt, besides a mortgage that we want to pay off in seven years or less. We want to learn to live on the smallest amount of money possible and save buckets and buckets of it along the way.

We now desire to buy another cottage with more land because I'm super greedy now that I have the gardener's bug. The current house we live in would be a rental.

How do we do all of this on a small income? Let's get into that in the next chapter, why don't we?

Chapter 7

When You Have Very Little Money to Work With

Today, Bali manages a gas station again. The boss we like so very much had an abandoned, run-down gas station in the town we now live in. He asked Bali to come on over and revitalize it. This is one of the reasons that we wound up in this town. Bali started working here and when I would visit him, I discovered that it had a peaceful, slower pace that where we lived at the time.

After the station was cleaned up and running well, it was sold. The new boss was just fine, but there has been some ongoing construction across the street for quite some time now. It has caused a lot of financial difficulty for the businesses and shops that line that street. The new boss cut everyone's hours, so even though Bali earns a decent amount of $14 per hour, he is now only bringing in $2,000 per month.

Some of you who live in other states and are reading this may be coughing and thinking, "That is a small fortune, little lady!" In another state it would be. In Northern California it is not. We are, according to government charts, right on the poverty level. House prices here start at $250K, and that is usually for a house needing work and not in the most charming neighborhood. We are even in the most affordable town in our area. We moved here because we were priced out of Sacramento (which *used* to also be the most affordable place to live).

This used to be a very affordable town, but as the Bay Area people push into Sacramento and raise the rents and housing market, the Sacramento natives are now coming down here. I've seen a big jump in housing prices in the two years we have resided here, like double. There is nothing under $300K- $400K in Sacramento now, unless you don't care about the street you live on, and you can do that "handyman's special" to the extreme.

I was looking at homes in the city yesterday, and what I notice and find ridiculous is that most newish homes are an average of 2,900 to over 3,000 sq. ft.! Homes have tripled in size, and a home that cost around $100K in 2012 now goes for around $400K just seven years later. Some of the houses are in even worse shape. But it's the market. I think it's far worse, far more out of control than it was back in 2008 when it all burst, crashed, or whatever it is that a housing market does.

Many people are forced to pay these exorbitant prices because California has had so many fires over the last few years, burning entire towns and suburbs to the ground. Thousands of people and families need housing. The market takes advantage of this desperation.

But we live well. We can live just fine on even less than $2,000 per month. Our mortgage, insurance, property taxes, and mortgage protection insurance total $933. We have inexpensive insurance, no car payments, and no debt. Well, except for the $124K remaining on the house.

We are no longer a one income family, however. I lost that claim a while back as my book royalties grew and I built and monetized my YouTube channel. I now bring in the missing amount from the hours that were cut at the gas station. We are thriving, but for a while, we weren't saving at all. I would write up budget after budget in my spiral notebook. I had pencils, a calculator, and colored highlighters. I wrote out breakdowns and budgets 1, 2, and 3. I stripped and cut out things like cable and the health club. We use graywater on the last patch of lawn remaining and never have lights on during the day. We even had solar panels installed on our roof. In the winter, I use our fabulous Presto Heat Dish heaters that hardly use any electricity.

But after we paid for the mortgage, utilities, gas for our vehicles, insurance premiums, and groceries, it seemed nothing was left to save.

We were doing it wrong. We would pay the mortgage and bills, and then use up all the rest for food, toiletries, and pet food. Then, if there was a little left over, we might go out for lunch, use extra gas, or get a mocha at the health food store, and sometimes buy convenience foods. The accounts would wind up overdrawn at the end of the month. I felt like a bit of a penny-pinching failure. My husband and I bickered. I had to find a way to be successful at household budgeting.

One day, I read a blog and there was something about paying yourself first. I ignored it. Then it came back around in another comment or article. I mulled it over. Then, something happened one month that forever changed the way I manage money.

I always pay my mortgage two weeks ahead of time, so when Bali mentioned a friend who was in need of a loan, I agreed to sacrifice our first paycheck of the month. Then, with the next paycheck, we had to pay for a big bill that could not wait. It took up most of that paycheck. We were left with only my small royalties to work with that month. We did it just fine. I had a decently stocked pantry and we got through with just a little bag of groceries that we bought around the middle of the month. I had beans and rice and plenty of flour to make all of our bread and tortillas. With the addition of potatoes, onions, some fruit, soy milk, and creamer, all was well. I had the mortgage paid the prior month and my royalties paid for the bills and insurance premiums. We drove very little and stayed home a lot.

This got my little mind a tickin' and I decided that this "pay yourself first" thing was smart. It turns out that this idea is from *The Richest Man in Babylon* by George S. Clason. The ladies on my channel keep me up to date on these things. I've ordered the book from the library, but still don't have it on hand so I can't review it at this time. Tony Robbins suggests everyone read this book so it must have some gems in it.

Now, this is what we do with our finances. Every month, the first paycheck goes into savings. The second paycheck pays the mortgage. My royalties pay for bills, groceries, gas, and any extras.

It's tight at times, but I have learned to live within our new budget. I'm not as quick to drive to the mountain town as I used to be. I combine errands and plan out trips. Stocking my pantry has almost become a side job. One woman described it as a hobby, and it inspired me. I have a very well-stocked pantry now. I've learned that ordering large amounts of flour, grains, beans, and such from the co-op is surprisingly inexpensive, even when it's all organic. I get oils and extras (all organic) at Grocery Outlet. At this time, we could easily go a month without shopping and still eat well.

Switching to a mostly plant-based diet and learning to make my own soy milk and faux meats are other huge money savers and great ways to avoid the store. I no longer need milk every five days. I just make my own!

Chicken and roast meat cost a pretty penny, especially when I decided to buy all clean meat: free range, without antibiotics or hormones. A chicken like that could cost $17 to $25. Now I make faux steaks and faux baloney. It costs nickels. We love it. It's not for everyone, and I realize this. I'm just happy that it works for us because our grocery bill went from around $800 - $1,000 per month, down to $300 just by making these changes.

I'll tell you what else saves us money big time: not going out, not eating out, not venturing out to see "what's happening out there," not nothing. We stay home.

You want some golden advice on how to save big? We pay ourselves first, right? Then we **force** ourselves to live on what is left. This means cutting out more stuff if we need to, finding more ways to use less, and finding more ways to stock our pantry on a set amount of grocery money. That is the other trick: having a set grocery amount. Force and set! It will make one a very creative and imaginative person, let me tell you.

When I'm intense and set on making it all work, we go nowhere and do nothing outside the home, unless it's free. Parks are free, so we spend hours at the park. We have three parks within easy walking distance. Walking our little Molly is free and if we walk down the more charming, tree-lined streets, it's very pleasurable. Sometimes we will walk all the way to Dad's station to visit.

Libraries are not only free, but they have toys and computers! We love the library and pick up stacks of great books that we can't wait to read every week. Think about it. You can go book shopping at the library every week and bring home top hits, new novels, and New York Times Best Sellers for free. You can also find a huge selection of movies, including new releases. We have mastered the library system thanks to a good librarian back in my Walnut Grove days. He taught me how to get online and order from many counties. We also recently began to take advantage of The Zip Book Project. We are able to order any book that costs less than $35 from Amazon. It will come straight to our home and after we've read it, we take it to the library to add to their collection. You can do this as many times as you'd like but only one book at a time. Sadly, not all libraries do this. I was hooked on a particular medieval romance series, but the books cost $16 each at the bookstore, so I ordered them from the library's Zip Book Project. I can order any desired book and it's like a gift in the mail. I do have to give it to the library in the end, but I don't often reread books anyway. The ones I feel like I will reread, I end up buying later.

I work on making the house as charming and cozy as possible, with nooks and areas for us all. The garden has been transformed into a fairy garden with chimes and stained glass ornaments that hang from trees. There are birdhouses, baths, feeders, trees for shade, and little fairy doors and wells set at tree bases. When I'm outside, the bird song is thick and the wind plays on my chimes. I love being out there in the spring, watering all the rows of tiny green plants, while I quiet my mind so I can fill it with the tinklings and chirpings.

In our home, I have taken to lighting a large scented candle on the table, and we always have music playing. Sometimes it's Pandora and sometimes it's my $2 thrifted radio that I keep in the laundry room.

Bali and I splurged last year and purchased an inexpensive, generic 40" Smart TV. It fits nicely in our oak cabinet and it isn't the focus of the living room. It always seems sad to me when I see a large TV over the fireplace. People used to display a large family portrait or a beautiful painting over the fireplace, and the mantle was decorated in lovely ways. Nowadays it's a big, ugly flat screen TV.

But I'm guilty of loving TV. I love a good movie, and especially a series. I was hooked something fierce on Downton Abbey, and then recently, I'm embarrassed to admit that I became hooked on three seasons of The 100 on Netflix, but I was over it when they killed off my Lincoln and Lexa. During my beloved Christmas season, I watch Christmas romances by the dozen. And don't even get me started on documentaries! It's my favorite way to learn. YouTube is my other favorite way to learn everything from gardening to cooking, all for free.

Writing is also free. I love to write, and every time I think I'm done with writing about homemaking, out pops another book or another blog post. Sometimes I just turn on my cell phone and make another video for YouTube. All of this is free, but writing and video-making also happen to bring in a little bit of income, so there is a bonus in those hobbies.

I used to be the kind of girl who had to keep going and running about. I would work all the time, and when I wasn't working, I'd either visit a friend or my treacherous mother. I drove millions of miles. I was always running from myself, trying to outrun my shadow, so to speak. I think back at all the life and energy I wasted; that could have been focused on something productive.

Another excerpt from Connie Hultquist's book, *Dear Kitchen Saints*:

"I mean, he is workin' like a dog to keep the family afloat and his wife is out running carefree all day? Wasting gas and money . . . that sure is not praising or honoring your husband as the priest of the home . . . it shows him no respect at all . . ."

I don't run around wasting money or gas anymore. My husband works long hours at a less than thrilling career. He never complains or bemoans his job. I'm sure that if he would be honest, he would rather be doing many other things, but he lies and says it's a job and he's happy to have it. So I make sure to use the money wisely. I try to make Bali proud but sometimes it's like trying to please a difficult parent. Since adopting the "pay yourself first" method, he is happy as a pig in a . . . in a . . . what is that saying? Oh, never mind.

Chapter 8

Decorating With Little or No Money

Yesterday was Monday, the beginning of a long week for most people. I was writing up a storm and slurping homemade lattes, feeling inspired. Not inspired enough to get out of my pajamas before 1 p.m., but who has time to shower and dress when there are deadlines and the creativity is flowing? Arjan and Sam were busy with their own projects of art and building.

I had a lovely woman write to me, saying that she had been thinking about the design of my house and was trying to figure out how to make two rooms for the children. We are in the process of becoming foster parents and if I take in girls, I need another bedroom. She thought we had three bedrooms, but we only have two. When I told her this, she went on to imagine something else for me. I enjoy when people reimagine my house. It gives it a fresh look and I love playing around with the rooms and furniture to make it look new and different. It also helps with deep cleaning.

The woman suggested that I combine the dining room and living room by moving the table and chairs into the living room area, then turn the original dining room into a snug little reading/art room. I pondered the idea, but it was when I discovered a huge pen leak on my lovely down comforter (because Arjan keeps creating art on his bed) that I decided that was it!

I spent part of my morning cooking, writing like mad, feeding children, and writing some more (NaNoWriMo deadline, you know). Then, I felt this surge of energy, probably from the espresso kicking in at last, and I began tackling the two rooms. I hauled and moved furniture this way and that, I rehung paintings, found more in my entryway closet, and I vacuumed and mopped.

The boys and I recently took Molly to a small field nearby and we found a table and some chairs on the street. I couldn't believe they were free because there was nothing wrong with them, except for one chair that was a bit wobbly. The round little table was made of oak and had leaves that could serve as a sideboard. We decided that if it was still there after we played, we would haul it home. At the field, Arjan ran Molly, and Sam followed behind. It's sort of like Arjan runs both Molly and Sam to wear them out. We watched one small car after another pull over and try to fit the table in their back seat or trunk. We held our breaths as they tried to squeeze it in, finally giving up and leaving our treasure. After the third car drove off, we decided it was time to rush home and retrieve our truck.

Now that little table and two cute chairs are in our living room, serving as a craft and art area. I've set it up with all the extra furniture, and we even set up our large, fancy, fake Christmas tree. We did it 10 days before Thanksgiving, which was breaking our tradition, but Sam has been begging me to decorate for Christmas for a good week now, so I agreed to at least do the tree.

And what a great tree this turned out to be! Arjan and I found this brand-new faux tree at a thrift store in Nevada City. It cost around $20. Now that I've unboxed it, I see that it is a really sturdy, quality tree. It's very thick and tall, probably around seven feet in height. If you shopped for a similar tree through a nice company such as Balsam Hill, it would be between $599 and $899. Yes, you can get a cheap one at Walmart or Target for $50 to $100, but we did that years ago and finally gave it away. It was a very Charlie Brown tree, if you know what I mean. Some of you may remember that Christmas special where Charlie Brown chose a sparse and sad little tree.

For the last couple of years, we have followed a family tradition of going to a tree lot after Thanksgiving and choosing a nice, thick tree. We decorate all day while we rock out to Christmas music, which doesn't stop until the day after Christmas. It is a serious affair around here. Christmas is my favorite time of year.

There are times that I will rearrange my furniture monthly, as I clean the house. I will move the whole sofa to the other side of the room, and the TV cabinet to the other side of the wall. Let me tell you, these are not IKEA pieces. This is an L-shaped sofa and a heavy, solid oak cabinet. I often need to see the chiropractor after these days of inspiration.

Every six months I'll switch the bedrooms. However, I think they are perfect now. The front bedroom fits the bunk beds for the boys and a queen-sized bed for guests. The back room is for Mom and Dad. It's off the kitchen so I can roll out of bed and be at the coffee pot within steps. Can't beat that.

When your house is 1,000 sq. ft. and has two bedrooms, you can only go so far. Despite its size, I've managed to work a hundred arrangements out of a space that you would think can only be arranged in five different ways.

I remember a woman sharing about how her grandmother (or great-grandmother) and her neighbor switched houses. They lived right across the road from each other and they both had simple homes and few belongings, so it wasn't a big deal. They thought it was great fun to switch homes, and I think they stayed in each other's houses for some time. Now *that* is creative. Then there was another story of a grandmother who made a bedroom out of her kitchen. I can't quite get my brain to create that scene but once again, very imaginative.

To me, a house is a grown-up dollhouse, a huge gift. It is to be enjoyed to the fullest, and to be played with. Every inch of the house and yard is to be used completely and to its full potential.

If you move into a small house, you learn how to be creative with shelves and storage. I made a full walk-in pantry out of my laundry room. I maximize space. A dining room is no longer just a dining room. It is a dining room, library, office, school, and art studio. Our bedroom closet easily stores my clothes, the boys' clothes, shoes and slippers for everyone, toys, a small carpet shampooer, and a vacuum. The kids' closet fits Bali's clothes (we never completed the switching of clothes when we changed rooms this last time), all my holiday and seasonal decor, two electric heaters, and my wooden clothes rack. The closets aren't jam-packed and they don't have things falling out when you open them. They are neat and tidy and have room for more things.

The living room is now the entertainment room, sitting room, and even has a little art/study area.

The kitchen is only the kitchen because it is stuffed and busy and would never share itself with anything else. The kitchen is a prima donna, but the heart of the house. She is a mass-producing little factory. I cook, bake, study recipes, store tons of food and kitchen tools, can, preserve, and dehydrate foods in that one room.

Today, we had a chiropractic appointment for Arjan and Sam. I also needed one, but I'm thinking of getting back to yoga to save myself $60 a month in visits. We checked our mailbox and found that two lovely ladies had sent me the most delightful, handmade recipe books. I'm eager to pore over them, but that will have to wait. I also received a little bit of cash from a generous soul. I went to Grocery Outlet and found a nice, small carpet for the kids' room, a pine-scented Christmas candle, and a small, leafless tree for the table. It is perfect for a craft idea we came up with after having lunch at our favorite Chinese restaurant the other day.

I collect decorating ideas everywhere I go: from magazines at doctors' offices, from our favorite restaurants, from movies, and from other homes in real life or ones that I see on YouTube videos. I collect a scrapbook of snapshots in my mind and then I begin to search for items at thrift stores in nice neighborhoods and make my way to side streets as I look for cast-offs to rescue.

Nothing matches in my house. It is very hygge/shabby chic, and I adore it.

People who come over always want to stay longer than planned. It's cozy here, and I'll feed you. I'll make a pot of coffee, we'll talk about whatever you feel needs to be explored, and I'll listen intently.

I have a friend who I've known since I was seven years old. She worked in my godfather's office for decades. Despite the fact that she is seven years older than me, we have been great friends for ages, and she is now one of my children's godmothers. I say one of the godmothers because they have two godmothers. Hey, they don't have any grandparents, so we must make up for that in other ways. This family of mine owns a million properties. Okay, maybe less than a hundred. When a tenant leaves, they always seem to leave something good behind and they gift it to me. One of these gifts was a crazy old lamp that I have in my living room. It is huge and green with a lampshade the size of a dwarf tree. They also gave me a fantastic Kirby vacuum cleaner that I use daily, compliments of apartment abandonment. Sometimes I score odd little pieces of art, as well.

One of my favorite tricks is tripling my houseplants. I have a lot of ivy-like plants and they are so easy to propagate. I trim off a branch, put it in a jar full of water, and place it on a sunny windowsill until I see delicate roots. I then transfer it to a pot or coffee can with soil, and within just a few months, I have a lush (free) plant!

I have funky taste. I love color, lots of color. I don't care for things to match. The more color and mismatched, the more delightful a room looks to me.

I start by painting the room a warm, rich color, then I add hand-me-down furniture or pieces I found for very little money at thrift stores or on Craigslist. I use colorful pillows and cloth or sheets to adorn sofas and chairs. I love hanging paintings of faraway villages and countrysides on my walls. I want to look at a painting and be carried away on vacation in my mind.

Smells are a big signature thing for a house. My house is old, and sometimes it smells like it. I have dogs that get smelly and boys who get sticky. So, I use a lot of scented wax, incense, candles, and homemade potpourri. When someone enters my home, I want them to smell cinnamon and cloves, pine, fresh laundry, or other delights. I don't want them to smell old dog, stinky boy, or 70-year-old house.

Chapter 9

Marriage, Motherhood, Being at Home, and Modern Society

I married my Punjabi Indian husband shortly before my 41st birthday. I also became pregnant just days before turning 41.

I spent my 30s crying and yelling at God for not fulfilling my dreams of becoming a mother. I wanted my babies and I wanted them at age 15. Well, even sooner than that, because I started exploring pregnancy and motherhood when I was just six or seven years old. I remember interrogating my second grade teacher's assistant about the act of birthing a baby. I wanted details. I wanted to know the length of time it took and the degree of pain that was involved. I also remember inspecting my chest and when I couldn't see "holes" in my nipples, I went crying to my mother and asked her how I would nurse my babies. I had no holes in my nipples! It's sort of embarrassing to share this now, but the point is that I was obsessed with my ability to have and nurse and tend to babies.

When I was about eight years old, I brought a baby home. My mother was a crazy lady most of the time, but she was cool this time. She also had a compassionate heart. The baby belonged to a homeless man who stayed on people's porches. Everyone gave him work, despite the fact that he wasn't too bright or capable. I asked him if I could bring his baby home and he agreed. I took care of her by myself all day and night. I can barely remember this anymore, so I can't tell you if it was just one night or a couple of days, and I don't remember how much my mother helped. I'm sure she *did* guide me somewhat, but she also let me tend to the baby on my own. I was a natural. I loved babies. I wanted one before I even became a woman. The baby I brought home was eventually adopted by our friends who had a loving home and two children of their own.

It would take 33 more long, toturesome years before I held my own bundle in my arms and suckled him at my bosom. I didn't put my first child down for months and months until he wiggled to be free. He clung to my chest and nursed for almost five years. It was only slight embarrassment that forced me to push him from the breast.

Now I have two boys who I'm so crazy in love with, and they are just as crazy about their mama. No matter where I go in the house, it isn't long before they find me and gather at my feet to continue playing. They want to be next to me all the time. It's heartwarming, and I must admit that my ego loves it all, until I want to go watch the latest Star Wars movie and suddenly everyone in the house has separation anxiety. It's a must that I silence my cell phone because Arjan will call me 10 times to beg and then demand I come home. It's not easy to carve out two hours of me-time.

I love the energy that children fill a home with. When it was just Bali and I, the house was tidy and easy to keep clean, but it was blah. Pretty, tidy, and blah. Now we have dinosaurs in the tub, dinosaurs in my potted plants, and dinosaurs in the yard. On our windowsills, we have leaves, pinecones, strange sticks, and amazing stones that we gathered during forest adventures. I have bottles of sand from visits to the beach. Our home is a shrine of sweet memories with our little boys, enthusiastic and curious about this planet and this life.

When Arjan was very little, around four years old, he used to say, "When I was your father…" I believe in reincarnation so I never ignored this. One day, we were at a big park on the Sacramento River. We were watching the men prune the large shade trees. Arjan said, "I used to do that when I was your father." He would say things like this every now and then. He later said that Sammy was my little brother in our other life and I was very good at taking care of him, and that was why he wanted to come back as my son. I believe it, seeing how attached Sam is to me. I believe it with Arjan as well because he has been lecturing me like an old man since he could talk. He acts like an old father in a tiny boy's body.

Motherhood comes naturally and feels like the arm I was missing my whole life. Now my life is complete, and I can think about other things now that my boys are with me. Perhaps my spirit knew these two were waiting for me and that caused the anxiety. But I had to get my life together before I had them. I wanted to be healthy mentally, physically, and spiritually. I wanted to have a good husband and a good father for them. Life had to be prepared for these little people.

Being Married

I very much enjoy being married. I spent 40 years out there in the world alone. Because my mother was mentally unstable, I took care of her from a young age, and then I floundered about in life, chasing happiness in the form of smoking too much pot. I chased it by moving often, and changing jobs every six to nine months. I was a mess for most of my life.

Then I discovered inner healing and transformed my life through a lot of inner work. I'm *still* doing the work and reaching new levels of happiness all the time. As I transformed my inner self, my outer self began to change, and I had a more positive life. I quit my habits and had a wonderful new life. But I was still longing for a companion.

Life isn't so easy on your own. There is the stress of always making rent and getting by, the night after night of crawling into a cold bed, and spending weekends alone because your friends are now married and have children. Then there's the tagging along with other families and feeling like that crazy aunt who lives alone with her cats.

When Bali showed up, I wasn't interested. I only fell for the wackadoos – the men who weren't stable, had addictions, and extra servings of issues. Oh, and they didn't stick around for very long. That is what I knew and liked. It felt just like home.

Bali was stable, younger than me, didn't have addictions, issues, or oddities. He had a good job. Boring. Besides, he was a foreigner, he wasn't fluent in English, and I was a talker. I liked men who were also funny and talked plenty, like me. Bali was the silent type. He wasn't funny and didn't get my jokes.

He pursued me for a good nine months until I finally gave in. I had asked God to send me a good man and said that I wouldn't fight it. I said that I wanted to be married within the next six to nine months. And that is what happened. I finally went out with Bali when I saw what a good person and a hard worker he was. We went out a few times and were married within a couple of months at a city hall. Two months later, we had a big garden wedding at a grange. We moved into another house the following month, and I was pregnant a month after that. Within just one year, I was married, a mother, and a housewife. I was thrilled!

There's been a lot of learning and improving over the years. Being a homemaker and mother comes naturally but I had no experience. I wasn't raised with a mother or grandmother who taught me how to clean properly, cook, get stains out of clothes, or to budget. I had to learn these things on my own.

It may sound silly, but all the jobs I had in my youth somewhat prepared me for my homemaking career. I had many restaurant and café jobs where I learned to clean, make coffee drinks, and prepare food. I learned about pantries, food storage, inventory, and rotation. I had office jobs where I learned to budget and organize, pay bills, file, and type. I had a housecleaning job, I babysat, and walked dogs. It all prepared me.

I only knew how to cook five main dishes back then. I could bake a chicken, make a delicious spaghetti sauce, amazing burritos, a chicken soup, and vegetarian bell pepper and black bean fajitas. I could also make a few side dishes like poached eggs, rice, and pasta. I knew how to make a house look clean and tidy, but I wasn't great at deep cleaning. I was tidy, but decluttering and really organizing (even proper clothes folding) weren't a reality yet.

I worked at a raw food culinary school before Bali and I got married. In the two years I was there, I worked in every department. This place really educated me on all matters of health and veganism. I learned to cook vegan soups made of vegetables like potatoes, leeks, and corn; to juice greens, make smoothies, and delicious salads. I learned about all sorts of kitchen tools and read books full of plant-based recipes and ideas. I then worked in the office, where all my organizing and secretarial skills surfaced. All of these experiences helped me to care for my family's health. The organization and money management skills were useful when we were saving money and buying our first house.

I'm a big YouTube person because I feel that it's taught me so much in many areas: cooking, cleaning, decluttering, organizing, gardening, homesteading, and spirituality.

The real education, however, began with this little fixer-upper house. Bali and I have both learned so much.

He learned how to DIY on a whole new level. Recently, our old car decided that the windows would not go up anymore. Bali went to the car dealership and was quoted over $500 for the repair, so he found the part on

Amazon and figured out how to install it himself. It works great . . . almost. One does have to roll up each window now, instead of the driver panel working all of them, but hey, it works and we saved a bundle.

He also found a free sink with counter someone was throwing away and installed it with the help of a YouTube video, and we haven't had one leak yet.

He can build fences and paint in a pretty professional manner, whereas I slop it about and must leave the trim and hard parts to him. We've both acquired some painting skills, but I'm better with large spaces without boundaries and he is skilled in the small edging of things.

We have learned so many things, from fixing the bottoms of old chairs, to refinishing wood floors, to gardening. We absolutely love gardening.

Bali and I have grown together with this house because it needed a lot of repairs and we learned how capable we are. We are both very hard workers. I'm more studious about it and he has the brawn to get in there and build it, dig it, or install it.

Together we have built a good home and life for our little family, and we have more love and respect for each other because of it.

My struggle now is in finding balance. I am very creative and love my writing and channel. However, I remember the time before I wrote books, made videos, had a blog, or had friends on YouTube. What I did then was simply be with my children, keep my house clean and tidy, cook simple meals, keep a good budget, grocery shop once a week, and read. I read novels back then, one after the other.

Now I keep ordering novels and sending them back partly read after two or three renewals. I have no time to really read a book anymore, so I skim.

I feel like I don't spend the same kind of time with my kids that I used to. I'm with them all day long and we go places and do things, but really sitting with them and being present is an area that is lacking. They want to *really* be with me. They want me to play, talk, and tell stories. Reading books to Sam in the morning, enjoying Arjan's art, or walking Molly, just doesn't feel deep enough. I know they want a deeper connection with me. I'm learning to balance my career with motherhood and homemaking. I'm learning to take vacations and slow down, to put my focus on what is most important: my beloved family.

I started writing because I wanted to share everything that I was learning, to show others that there is a better way. There is a way to have the charming home without needing a vast amount of money, to have a good, rich, luxurious life without working yourself to death. I wanted to show men and women that a parent can stay home, and it is possible even in this crazy economy. I wanted to teach the parents at home that it doesn't have to be lonely and boring. It doesn't have to be depressing or feel like drudgery.

I started my YouTube channel for the same reason. There was a time when my children wanted to be close to me all the time, but didn't need me to be so engaged. When they are little tots they are exploring and just need you nearby, but not on their little heads about everything. Arjan loved playing quietly for hours, and if I'd intruded, talking at him the whole time, he might have thrown sand at me to silence the chatter. Sam just wanted to be nursed and cuddled, then explore peacefully.

Now they want interaction. They have stories to tell. Sam sings songs and tells stories that go on forever, and we must beg him to save it for the next day. Arjan wants to talk about everything he is learning. We call him "Facts and Figures."

So now I'm looking at making changes in my self-made careers, so that I have the time to focus on the little men in my life before they hit puberty and want little to do with me.

One way to do that is to have faith in my husband's income. There used to be a time when a woman worked the home and tended the children and there was no part-time work or side hustle. Yes, she may have made jam or baked a pie and sold it for extra change, so I suppose there has always been a bit of a side hustle. But the wife would just make more of what she was already doing; more jam-making or baking to sell the extra.

Nowadays there are all sorts of side hustles and work-from-home gigs. Women will run themselves ragged trying to get a website or a blog to be profitable. They turn a nice hobby into a corporation. Then there is YouTube. I see a woman start out humbly sharing her home, recipes, and cleaning routine, and then she builds her channel up to tens of thousands of subscribers, and now she's selling this and that, being sponsored by this product and that company.

I read about mothers of infants and children getting so stressed out. This is not good at all.

I love reading books by Mrs. Sharon White and Connie Hultquist. I have a stack of Mrs. Sharon White's books including *Living on His Income: Remembrances and Advice for the Christian Housewife, Introduction to Home Economics: Gentle Instruction to Find Joy in Christian Homemaking, An Old Fashioned Budget: Humble Financial Management for the Christian Housewife,* and more. I also have Connie Hultquist's *Dear Kitchen Saints*, which I've previously mentioned in this book.

I enjoy reading both of these ladies' books because they support and encourage me to embrace and surrender to this life at home. They talk of letting the man be a man and provide fully and deal with the finances. They talk of being content in one's housework and spending time with the children. It reminds me that my longing is being in my home, and that I don't want to create stress for myself or my family, or live like everyone else in this modern world.

Living on His Income: Remembrances and Advice for the Christian Housewife is a wonderful reflection of Mrs. Sharon White's life as a homemaker. She tells stories of how her mother, aunt, grandmother, and mother-in-law kept a home. They all had slightly different styles, but the theme is the same. None of them had a lot of money but they took very good care of what they had. Their pride was in having a clean and tidy home, in cooking nourishing meals and keeping their family well-fed. The women were careful with the household money and made the grocery funds stretch.

All of them stayed home. They didn't run around with friends, go to luncheons, or shop. They didn't work or find side jobs for extra money. Their job was to create a nice home from what they had and support their husbands, love their children and make do.

It seems that they were content and satisfied with their lives.

I often have women write to me, talking about being stressed, lonely, or bored. They are tired of the frugal life.

I do understand. I'm sure the mothers of the past had bouts of loneliness and at times felt tired of being poor. Bored? I sort of doubt that. If we are talking about old time mothers, there was the hand-washing of clothes, scrubbing of floors on hands and knees, gardening, and canning food for the winter in order to survive. There wasn't time to be bored.

Our modern world is full of consumerism. There is advertising everywhere: on the streets, driving down the highway, on the Internet. I can't even read someone's blog without videos and banners popping up here and there, blocking the article. We have Black Friday shopping as a tradition now and malls are everywhere. There are so many online shopping options – Amazon, Overstock, Wayfair, and on and on.

We have credit cards for instant gratification and loans for cars and homes. We don't have to wait for anything, do we? Swipe it, sign on the dotted line, and it's "yours."

We don't know what it's like to save for a pair of shoes, then order them, and wait a few weeks. Amazon will give you a credit card and send those shoes to you the very next day if you're a Prime member.

I truly believe that the problem with many people's lack of joy and satisfaction is not in their marriage, job, or even life. It is from overstimulation on a mass level; from addictions, bad habits, and instant gratification.

I feel that the solution is pulling away from this modern life on a huge scale, by getting off media, cutting up the credit cards, turning off the news, overcoming the addiction to drinking, pills, shopping, or whatever, and slowing way, way down in life.

With everyone working, we have created this crazy pace, crazy housing market, and unhappy, empty homes.

You may say, "Kate, you're so simple." No, I really think that the solution to most of our societal problems is to have a parent at home, regardless of gender; whoever it is that does the best job and will take it up with both hands and nurture the project. And to get off the mainstream. Delete your Facebook account. If a cousin is getting married, they will send an invitation. If something important happens with a family member or friend, they will call . . . or should. You won't miss anything but comparing yourself to people's fake

Facebook lives. You will avoid jealousy, hurt, envy, and coveting. No more political arguments!

Get off Twitter. It's mindless, and the fact that people argue on it publicly is enough to tell you it isn't a good place.

Delete your Instagram account. Who cares what others are doing? Go do something and enjoy your own life.

They are all addictions. I watched a TED Talks video about this. Facebook, Twitter, Instagram . . . all these social media platforms have what they call Happiness Engineers. They are the same people that research and find ways to get people addicted to slot machines and games in Las Vegas. They are hired by casinos to find ways to keep people coming back. They are also hired by these media platforms to find ways to keep you hooked. All the thumbs up, the views, and happy comments are designed to keep your attention. "Way to go, Mary! You have all these views. Everyone loves your stuff!" People become like rats hitting that release button, posting things just to see how many thumbs up, views, and comments they get.

This drives people. They are no longer present. They aren't in the real world, with real people who are sitting at the table with them.

Did you know that many CEOs of companies like this won't let their children have accounts or iPads? They know about the addictions and dangers.

Chamath Palihapitiya is a former Facebook executive, and now talks very strongly about the guilt he feels for the role he had in helping to build the company. He feels that it is tearing the very fabric of our society in so many ways.

Steve Jobs wouldn't allow iPads in his home because he felt they were too dangerous for his kids. Interesting.

It's time to wake up. We are addicted and the companies love it. Just like how cigarettes used to be good for digestion, right?

Once you give yourself a month or more to detox (including the news) and stop missing it, you will see a balance take place and a peace settle over your soul. You will feel much less nervous. You may even lose that depression. It may take extra work because you've taken in the news and political feeds for so long that you might have a little PTSD. You will need some heavy detoxification of the soul and mind.

My advice is to turn to funny movies or old sitcoms. Read good books and listen to good music to fill in what will become a big void. You must replace a habit with another habit, or you will go right back to the original, or find an equally awful one (e.g. getting sober and then taking up a shopping addiction).

Let's put our energy and focus back on our children and home. Focus on the marriage and what is good in our lives.

Chapter 10

The Zen Home

I deleted my Facebook account a few months back and I don't miss it at all. I also deleted Twitter, Instagram, and some other stuff like LinkedIn, and things that I didn't understand but had used to promote my books years ago.

The news are not allowed in this house, unless we are having major fires and floods, and then we tune in now and then to keep updated in case we must evacuate. I usually keep my radio on for emergency announcements.

Other than that, I fill our home with all that is fun, lovely, calming, healing, or for growth. I have shelves of books on homemaking, spiritual work, gardening, and canning.

On Pandora, I have many different genres of music: country, reiki/meditation/yoga, Native American, classical, gospel, contemporary Christian, dance, and children's music, to name a few.

I always have some coffee brewing in the morning and sometimes, if I'm doing lots of cleaning or decorating a room, I'll make a little pot in the afternoon. I keep things fresh by moving furnishings and paintings around. In addition to an abundance of rose bushes, I grew some lavender outside the kitchen, allowing me to have a lovely bouquet anytime. I will often grab a basket and fill it with various roses in yellow, lavender, pink, red, and white. I'll put small vases with fragrant roses in each room. Other times, I'll use lavender instead.

I've tried the very stripped-down minimalist look in my home, but promptly brought everything back in and added more shelving, colors, and pillows. I like a cozy look; however, I like a very clean house as well, and it takes a bit more work when it's busy with furnishings and decorations.

Every morning, I fully open my blinds to let in as much light as possible. I light my scented candles or turn on my wax warmers and let the fragrances permeate the air. There are controversies surrounding the safety of scented candles, but I live right in the middle of farmland and breathe in pesticides daily, so a little emission from a scented candle is the least of my worries. Other times, when I want to switch things up, I will place a small pot on the back burner of my stove and fill it with water, cinnamon sticks, and cloves for a delicious fall spice scent. I love seasonally scented candles just like I love seasonal coffee. In the spring, I like to use fresh laundry scents, tropical in the summer, cinnamon spice in the fall, pumpkin pie in November, and pine tree in December. When it comes to coffee, I love my pumpkin spice lattes and peppermint mochas. I don't know that I've discovered my spring and summer drinks yet. Perhaps iced coffee in the summer. In warmer seasons, I like to open all the windows to let in the sun and air, and to hear the marvelous sound of chirping birds.

I make the beds first thing in the morning and wash any dishes that magically appeared in the sink after the last kitchen clean-up the night before. Then I may make some toast or simmer a small pot of steel cut oats for the children.

If I've read some books to Sam, I'll then get on my laptop to check my stats and email, respond to comments on my channel, or upload a new video. I may begin my writing.

Spring is one of my favorite seasons. I so enjoy planting my summer crop and preparing my seedlings to go out into the garden. I used some of my royalty money last year and bought myself a little greenhouse that has served us well. I had never attempted to grow seedlings, but I did some research and started the journey in February of that year. I did everything I learned: water daily, but not too much, start feeding the babies once they get their first leaves, cut the fertilizers in half, then when the time comes to plant, start putting them outside a little at a time for a week until they have hardened off.

I had fantastic luck and grew huge tomato plants that almost turned into trees. I harvested tomatoes for sandwiches, sauces, and salads, and in the end, I made quarts and quarts of spaghetti/pizza sauce. I harvested piles of butternut squash, honeydew melons, eggplants, zucchini, and bell peppers. I was thrilled and proud.

But there's something magical about the very beginning when I plant seeds in the ground, and I stand in my lush and lovely garden in the morning, listening to the sound of chimes tinkling gently among the branches, my finches thick in the camellias. I water by hand and I feel peace and calm. I love visiting and seeing the tiny sprouts making their way up from the earth, getting bigger and stronger each day. Then there are the days when I come out to water my plants and some bug has been having a delicate salad with my new sprouts.

I spend entire days in my kitchen rolling out dough, putting together soups or casseroles, and watching cooking shows while I follow along. I love to do some bulk cooking, making plenty of food to last for days. This is great when I have a writing project that I'm working on. In the past, I would bake a couple of chickens and a few loaves of bread, simmer a big pot of beans, steam a pot of rice, and roast a pan of potatoes.

That would feed us for days and we could mix and match, adding either a quick pan of sautéed vegetables or a salad to complete the meal. Now that we are back to eating plant-based, I will make two lentil loaves, a big pot of mashed potatoes, a huge salad, a few loaves of wheat bread, a gallon of soy milk, and a glob of gluten to make faux steaks, bologna, and "chicken" nuggets. I will then add piles of vegetables or a huge salad. I like to finish some of these dishes off with some mushroom gravy for extra flavor, too. This feeds us for days.

Feeding my family organic foods that are wholesome and filling feels good to me. I'm ensuring the best possible health for us now and into the future. My children are not restricted at all, and if they are craving chicken or fish, goat milk, or eggs, they get it, but it's all clean and organic, possibly local and compassionately raised. Thank goodness we don't serve much of that because it is very expensive to have clean food that was raised with kindness.

Creating a sweet ambiance at home raises the vibration and we are all content most of the time. Children will bicker and quibble over silly things no matter how mellow you make the atmosphere.

Our true focus at home is enjoying life, finding our dreams, and working toward them with full passion. For Arjan, that is his art and learning. He loves to read and hone his skills, sketching dinosaurs and their habitats. He loves to learn about animals and nature, science and odd facts. For Sam, joy comes in pretending he's Godzilla, creating stories in his mind, and being read to. For me, it's playing with my home, creating in the kitchen, listening to Dr. Joe Dispenza or similar lecturers, writing books, blog posts, and making videos in which I share my knowledge and discoveries.

I also love grocery shopping at the health food store and trying new vegan products or sauces. I love coming home from the library carrying stacks of books to read. I love that short time right after deep cleaning the whole house when it feels so clean and fresh.

With two boys and three furry dogs, it's not easy to keep a home clean. There's hair, toys, pens, books, and more hair everywhere. I need a clean home for mental clarity. I work much better when my environment is clean and things are in order. I have found ways to keep it nice with little effort and short periods of work. I don't spend all day cleaning. I will sometimes work very hard one day and take a couple of days off with just light chores here and there. I've learned to be quick and clever with my routines or I would burn myself right out.

I must also keep myself inspired. I found a lady on YouTube who shows her cleaning routine. I love this lady as she really has the worst house by the time she cleans it. It looks like a bomb went off with her husband and five children. She speeds up the video and you can watch her magically clean her house from top to bottom and transform it from a crazy, wild mess to a sparkling, tidy home. I will watch one of her videos if I feel pooped out and have a day of cleaning ahead of me. After seeing what she is contending with and how she manages to make magical cleaning happen, I pour another cup of joe and get to work. Loud music helps.

Two channels I highly recommend for a more Zen-like experience in homemaking and cooking are *Haegreendal* and *Ivy Kitchen*. Both are based in Asian countries and have beautiful cinematography and editing. The videos are of the DITL (Day In The Life) variety, but you feel so peaceful and renewed after watching, making you want to slow down and embrace the simplicity of daily routines. These women remind me that everything we do can be made into a ritual, be it housecleaning, cooking, or raising a child. It is all a ritual and should be done with love and ceremony.

Many women will agree with me that cleaning is therapy. When we clean, we work through our issues. We start fights or make amends in our heads, we figure out our deep reasoning behind choices we've made, or find our true thoughts on yesterday's topics. We scrub away the problems, pour bleach on life's stains, and throw away our personal garbage. We declutter what doesn't work for us anymore, and rid ourselves of other problems. We set things right, get our priorities straight, finding clarity in it all.

At the end of a few intense hours or a whole day of this, we come out of it exhausted and our house is set right. I always feel good after a deep and exhilarating housecleaning session.

I feel good when I cook. I love trying new things and have fun learning how to veganize our favorite dishes. I enjoy watching other women make good, down-home food. But I really like the real videos, not the polished ones with high tech music in the background and superb editing. I do like those as well and will watch for convenience when trying to figure things out, but it is the videos where you feel like you are in their home with them, learning to cook or watching them clean that I enjoy the most. *Simply Sara Kitchen* on YouTube used to have short, cozy cooking videos of just her cooking at the stove. I have enjoyed many of her dishes: her minestrone soup, mushroom stroganoff, vegan corn dogs, and much more. She does a lot of vegetarian and vegan cooking these days, but the videos are streamed live, which makes it hard for me to cook with her now.

When evening falls, I have a warm lamp on in the living room, with another one wherever the kids are playing. They play or watch a movie after supper and a hot shower, and I curl up on the sofa in my pajamas and watch a movie. I usually skim a book or do a little work while watching a movie, unless it's a good one that hooks me.

A fun series that I've enjoyed is *Parks and Recreation* on Netflix. It is the sort of series that you think about the next day and it still makes you laugh, like when you had a good time with a friend the night before and you're still laughing at the fun moments.

It's good for the soul to have a snug night with funny shows, books that you can skim without fully having to commit, and being surrounded by little people and maybe a little dog to cuddle with on the sofa.

Chapter 11

How to Build a Home and Life on a Small Budget

I saved the best for last. I love figuring out how to live on a small budget. I much prefer to learn from a family who is on hard times, living in a trailer and on food stamps, than a middle-class family with working parents, living in a large new house in suburbia. Or how about a middle-class family who hit hard times, took in a tenant, started baking their own bread, biking to work, and turned their suburban backyard into a small farm? Yes, those are my kind of people.

Why do I like the small and simple life more than studying wealth? I ask myself this often. I'm truly fascinated with the Connie Hultquists of the world. It just feels warmer, cozier . . . more *real*. I truly love the simple life.

I had a friend who passed away when Sam was born. Betty was my poor friend and had lived on welfare and disability for some time, but things weren't always like that for her. She used to work very hard and ran a busy daycare for many years in order to support her family, but then things got tough. There was the divorce that needed to happen, raising her children without child support, and a chronic illness, among other difficult things. I learned so much from her and her ability to continue living in the same house for years, to make lovely holiday memories for her two children, and to make their house a home. She knew how to make things happen and pinch a penny until it cried for mercy.

Betty was the best example of someone who had many challenges but made it all work out. She went from having a breadwinning husband and a successful daycare to being divorced, with no source of income or child support, and then becoming chronically ill with an autoimmune disease. Fortunately, she did receive a bit of government help and learned to work with small amounts of money. But the food stamps were limited, and the amount she was allotted to pay bills and everything else, such as gas and toiletries, was around $500. She was very fortunate to have all the assistance she received, and she took nothing for granted. But I think that we can all agree that living on $500 per month for bills, toiletries, gas, emergencies, along with birthdays for children, holidays, etc., takes a lot of creativity and planning.

Her children had no idea how much she struggled or that they were poor, and that is how it should be. Thanks to their mother, they were able to enjoy their childhoods without worry.

After her divorce, she stayed in the same house and applied for and received rent assistance. She never moved until the last two years of her life, but only because the landlord decided to sell the house.

The wall to wall carpeting was old, never having been replaced the whole time she lived there. The kitchen floor sagged. However, Betty kept her home very clean, shampooing the carpets whenever she could borrow a shampooer from a friend or a family member. She would throw area rugs over worn parts of the floor.

Her furniture was as old as the house, but she would cover the recliners and sofas with colorful afghans that her grandmother had crocheted decades ago. She kept a tablecloth and candle on her old table. In her bathroom, she had a collection of scented lotions, soaps, and shampoos that she would collect every time there was an incredible sale at the local Grocery Outlet or a thrift store. She often found candles of all shapes and sizes for only $0.10.

She always had a small scented candle in the bathroom when there were guests, and a large scented candle on the dining table.

During the holidays, there was always a spread on the table. For Easter, she would serve ham. For Thanksgiving and Christmas, she had a turkey.

She would start stocking up right after Thanksgiving, and especially after Christmas when stores had big sales. Since she didn't have a pantry, she would store boxes of food under her bed. They would be full of all the things she used to bake treats and cookies for her Christmas plates: sugar, flour, marshmallows, chocolate chips, candy canes, nuts, cans of condensed milk, and much more. She would start collecting little items for her children's stockings, usually from the dollar store.

She and her family had belonged to a church for decades and she would receive help from them from time to time. Her parents also helped her by buying extra toilet tissue when they would go to Costco. Sometimes they would buy a large package of huge muffins in a variety of flavors for her and her children. When her parents bought a turkey during the two-for-one sale, they gave her one. Betty had a deep freezer in her basement and would stock up turkeys or hams when she received someone's extra purchase. She was also generous and if she had extra turkeys and heard of someone in need, she would give them one, adding any other food or supplies she could find.

She wanted her children to go to a private Catholic school but couldn't afford the tuition. She either entered a rally or applied for scholarships; I can't remember, but I do recall both of her children going to this private school for all their schooling years and she never paid a dime. She was always winning or manifesting just what she needed at the time.

I remember her TV dying. She only had an antenna, but it didn't matter. It was sad because she was home often and it was her one guilty pleasure. Someone was getting rid of a big, flat screen TV, and her friends brought it to her. She was elated.

Like me, she also loved coffee. It was her favorite elixir. She would buy large cans of Folgers, or whatever dirt cheap brand she could find. She just used milk or cheap creamer and sugar.

I don't know if she ever went to a food bank, she never mentioned that. She did shop at FoodMaxx and Grocery Outlet often, and would call me and tell me of these fantastic shopping trips. She would find every sale in the store and build her pantry from that. I don't recall if she used coupons. Her kids probably ate free meals at school to help with stretching the budget. I do remember that she could take $50 in food stamps and come out with four full bags of groceries for the month. I'm not saying it was all super healthy, but when you are broke as broke can be and have little mouths to feed, you do the best you can (as nutritiously and frugally as possible), and stock up so you won't run out at the end of the month.

Betty was the one who taught me to save every gift bag, piece of tissue paper, string, and ribbon that I came across. She taught me to buy discounted packs of greeting cards or get them at a thrift store for just a few cents. Another friend taught me to create a stationary and gift wrapping box by putting all of those items inside a tub or large bag. When a holiday or birthday comes around, all I do is find the gift since I already have everything else. I donate to a few non-profit organizations and they will occasionally send me greeting cards that I save. If I find a pack for a dollar, I stock up. I send thank-you cards all the time for all the sweet gifts people send me.

That is how my friend Betty lived, but I didn't really pay much attention until our family moved and Bali took on a cashier's job with a huge pay cut. I wasn't working and we had no roommate.

I would call her and ask for tons of advice. I also recalled things that she had done in the past to help me know what to do.

It was seeing her get by on such a small amount of money and making it work that inspired me, and even now, when things are tight or we are trying to save money quickly, I think about her. It makes me feel grateful that we don't struggle as much as she did, and it helps me to implement all that she taught me while we save all that we can.

When you don't have much money to work with and have children you want to create a good childhood for, free of worry or hunger, and you still want a cozy home, you learn to be creative. You learn from others who have been at it for decades, whose homes are sweet and warm beyond words. You learn from those friends whose frugal food is not only delicious, but it also sticks to the ribs.

When you don't have a lot of money you learn to find the pleasures in life. You learn to stop running about and instead, settle into your home. Once you learn to settle into the home, you begin to fix it up, making it warm and cheerful. You learn to fill your days with homemaking and to enjoy it, taking pleasure in it. You learn to save money, and when you start finding incredible deals or find a good piece of furniture on the side of the road, you feel exhilarated and victorious. The little things become big things and life takes on new meaning. You begin to see the blessings in everything and cherish the simplicity of life's natural gifts.

A wealthy life seems boring to me. People make good money and buy a house that's too big (in my opinion). Then they buy the new cars, which leads to needing more money and a bigger promotion, and the greed begins to soar. Everything becomes about money. If it's all about money, it becomes an empty life with only one empty and meaningless goal: more money and more stuff.

Am I saying that poverty makes the man or woman? No. I'm saying that having a simple life can bring out the true meaning in life if you aren't focused on stuff and money. You can only truly understand this if you've decided to live a sustainable life, as we have.

I used to have dreams of a big house and nice things. I wanted to write incredible fiction and have a bigger life for my family. But then we bought this home and fixed it up, and I realized that what I truly wanted was stability. Owning a home brings stability, especially if it's affordable and you have a very small mortgage.

I enjoy learning from all the women who have made things work with their husbands' small paychecks. It helps me to respect our funds and make sure that I use our money wisely. A wife or partner needs to respect the hard-earned money and make sure that it pays all the bills and groceries, *at least.* If you can save some as well, then bravo! But to have your spouse work so hard and waste the family money is awful. It's not a good thing for a family to have a foolish person working the purse strings.

I haven't always been so wise with money. I buried myself in approximately $40,000 of debt in my late 20s and early 30s. I paid every penny back, but it took six years of working two solid jobs, adding a third job around the holidays, and living on a shoestring budget. Then, in my late 30s, I inherited two chunks of money which I used to pay off the remaining balance of a school loan and a used car I had financed, making me officially debt free.

It was wonderful, but I was not smart with the remainder of my inheritance. I just lived well, paid too much rent, took a less than stellar cruise, and enjoyed life working one part-time job. I felt that I deserved it, but I was foolish in my thinking. I wound up with nothing to show for all that spending. I could have purchased a little fixer-upper or done something with the money to make it count. Instead, I wound up broke after just two years.

I've learned my lessons. Bali and I have made some mistakes as well, but we straightened up fast. We look back and assess what we could have done differently. Take our house, for example. We now see that we could have saved thousands of dollars if we hadn't gone overboard with prettying it up. When we lived in Sacramento and were saving $600 per month after downsizing our lives, we could have put that money away in our savings account. But we just spent it.

I think about this and then bury myself in a book by Connie Hultquist or Mrs. Sharon White. Sometimes I just go to the end of *The Complete Tightwad Gazette* to read the success stories. I set goals and challenges to make it fun. I try new ideas all the time and anytime I hear of a frugal book, I quickly add it to my library list.

Our family is very fortunate. When our income was cut in half, we already had plenty. We still do. We now have some money coming in from my royalties, and I'm forever grateful that a hobby I love turned into a little bit of grocery money. I never saw that happening. We are fortunate to have a small mortgage and an easy life, but it took time and lots of learning. This life took strategy. The good choices we make today ensure a bountiful harvest in the future.

In order for us to continue saving money and reaching other goals, we must continue to live frugally. The good thing is that we truly enjoy living this way. After a while, you begin to feel satisfied with sunny days and good health. I admit that I do love to shop, but it has become less desirable lately. I have walked out of a few thrift stores without a thing in my basket, and that, my friends, is a miracle. The thing is, I feel full. I feel like there is nothing that I need or want. It's a great place to be.

The smart thing to do is keep that feeling and then take the time to find great deals on things we use and stock up. When you are not driven to shop, you shop slowly, wisely, with consideration.

When I'm given money now, I sit with it for some time. I think about what the family, the house, or the pantry may need, and how the money can serve us in the best way possible.

When I was blessed with some money recently, I let it sit in my bank for a few days, wanting to savor the feeling of abundance and deep appreciation for the gift. I wanted to use every penny as carefully and as wisely as possible. This was someone's money that they so generously gave me, instead of spending it on themselves. It was important to show just how much gratitude I felt to the person, to God, to the Universe.

I decided to stock my pantry with a variety of organic bulk foods. I paid for a 12-month subscription to ABCmouse for my sons' education, as well as one for Office Home & Student for my writing. I stocked our bathroom pantry with toiletries, and also bought some snacks and toys for our dogs.

In the past, I would have just run about and blown the money on dinners at restaurants, a thrift store spree, new books, and going out. I have children and a family now. Each penny is spent for all of us.

After Christmas is over, I will be embarking on another season of not spending. Starting with the first day of the new year, we will pay the mortgage, bills, and buy groceries and gas. Obviously, any emergency veterinary or car repair bill will be paid also.

This is a great way to save money quickly or get your budget in order again. If we are overspending and accruing some debt, a few months of no extra spending will straighten it all up. But it requires some devotion and constant motivation. I set a goal and remind myself often.

Connie Hultquist is another person who has struggled in life, but made sure that her children had a happy childhood, no matter how difficult things got.

She had a husband who had wandering feet for the first 12 years of their marriage. Jim would just disappear and not come home for months. Other times, he would wind up in prison. He made life a bit of a hell for this woman but she never lost faith in him, and eventually he was saved by God. They went on to enjoy 26 years of a good marriage and he became a good provider, father, and husband. Connie's book *Dear Kitchen Saints* is a collection of many years of her email writing ministry. At the end of the book, she includes her marriage testimony, which was very popular when it was printed in *Above Rubies Magazine* in September 2000. She shares the struggles that she overcame, and how she remained strong and made a life for her children when Jim wasn't there for them.

I recently read her book *Dear Christmas Mothers* and enjoyed it very much. I liked to read it aloud to my boys in the mornings, who enjoyed it too.

Connie writes about how she learned to make her own flavored coffees using instant coffee, powdered creamer, sugar, and maybe a packet of vanilla flavored pudding mix. She would make powdered cocoa mix by adding cocoa, sugar, and powdered milk to a 1-gallon glass jar. She made sugar cookies to give as Christmas gifts, and used old coffee cans to decorate.

You can use things in your home to make everything. Depression Era memoirs teach us that. In *We Had Everything but Money*, there are stories of mothers who had to make a home out of old farm shacks or chicken coops.

One woman was particularly amazing. She had to make it in a drafty old farmhouse with no money and what seemed like no furniture. She went down to the riverbed and hauled up clay, using it to plaster her walls to make them look nicer and keep the wind and cold out. Then she made a sofa out of an old, stripped box spring that she had cut in half with an axe, stuffing it with cotton that she picked herself, and covered it in fabric. She even managed to bring running water into the house using a basin and an outdoor hose.

The food they ate during the Depression was much simpler than today's fancy salads and roasted meats. Their main staples were beans, fried potatoes, and homemade bread. For dessert, they would maybe have some pie or just a spoonful of peanut butter drizzled with a touch of honey.

They would cover their walls with flour sacks or newspaper to keep the warmth in. I'm sure that families were just grateful to have shelter for their children. The women would decorate with what they had from their dowries or what had been handed down from parents and grandparents.

Having the ability to grow food was the big thing. With hardly any stores around, very little work, and not much money, people had to grow food to survive. They would plant up every inch with vegetables, and if they owned the property, they may have planted fruit trees as well. They would have chickens, and if they could, a cow. Maybe pigs.

Women canned and dried food like crazy. Men would smoke meat. Food had to be stored up for the winter. They were their only grocery mart.

I would not want this life, but I love to read about it and I'm more inspired than ever to grow as much of our food as possible. If times were hard, I'd snap out of it and start raising chickens and pigs, maybe a goat or two. But I don't have to get that heavy.

When we had our little Arjan and we noticed that the Circle K where Bali worked might be going under, I really started to manage our money differently.

I started the process of becoming licensed as a daycare provider and bought what I needed for it at thrift stores and on Craigslist. I didn't want to go back to work and leave Arjan with anyone, not even his father. I was nursing and he was so little. I trusted his father, but I had no luck pumping my milk and I was obsessed with nursing. The only way I could help us with money and stay home was to have a daycare.

Getting licensed was as easy as taking an online class that took about four hours, filling out paperwork that included diagrams of our house and yard, writing out emergency plans, and providing family information. Bali and I were fingerprinted, passed background checks, and had TB tests done. We took classes in first aid, health and safety, and CPR for Infants and Children. We also had our home inspected.

The fun part was building the daycare. I already had a crib that Arjan never slept in and a little playpen, but I needed high chairs and toys.

At thrift stores, I bought piles of stuffed animals and dolls, big stacks of children's books, blocks, and toys. I washed the stuffed animals in hot water and strong detergent, cut off tags and made sure they didn't have buttons that babies and kids could pull of and choke on. I had a book about house childproofing. I childproofed that house and all my houses since, from rafter to floor.

The child care agency I was working with had given me a box filled with files to keep organized, some books for kids, and books about cleaning and keeping the daycare safe. I read through it all, and to this day, I know what to do to have the safest home on the block.

I wiped down books with disinfectant and learned how to wash toys in the dishwasher by putting a soft screen over the racks and piling on the toys, then running through a hot cycle. This is a great way to clean a lot of toys at once, with hot water and good soap. I did this often during the cold and flu season.

I once had the best haul ever. I found a dollhouse and other items for sale on Craigslist. Bali and I only had a Toyota Corolla at the time, but we could really haul things if we were determined. We drove over the hill to a town in Redwood Valley to see the items, and I was thrilled. For $200 I pretty much stocked my daycare. There was a fantastic dollhouse with a big toy family and hundreds of pieces of furnishings, dishes, videos, rugs, even little newspapers, and more. You just can't find that anymore. They also gave me a little carpenter's station with plastic tools; and a kitchenette with boxes of plastic pots, pans, dishes, and foods. I was in heaven setting it all up, cleaning it, and playing with it all. I think I began the return to a better childhood right then and there.

The very day Bali closed the doors on his shop, a once thriving store and now a depressing, quiet shell, I got a call from a mother needing childcare for her four children. It was perfect. I had a whole family, full-time. I joined the food program to help with grocery reimbursement and with that little family and our roommate we were able to pay the rent, bills, gas, and groceries.

Bali helped a bit for the time we ran the daycare, but I did the majority of the cleaning, laundry, shopping, and caring for every child. To make life easier, I had a system.

I did most of the shopping once a month. I would save our roommate's rent money for the groceries. It totaled $500. We only had two markets in Fort Bragg, California: Safeway and Harvest Market. I loved

Harvest Market, but it was very, very pricey. You paid for the atmosphere and some organics. Safeway was also expensive. It was on the coast and everything costs more since it has to be trucked in on narrow, winding roads over many mountains. It took an hour to get to the small town of Willits and a couple of hours to drive to Ukiah, the nearest city.

On shopping day, Bali, Arjan, and I would head out to the store. It was no fun since Arjan detested being in his car seat or any type of stroller or carrier. He would howl and I would see Bali racing the grocery cart past aisles, trying to soothe him with a ride in the cart. I would shop fast! I knew exactly what my monthly menu was and what food supplies I needed. I cooked from scratch and I was able to feed all of us all month, roommate and children included, on this basic grocery list.

It went a little something like this:

Four packets of grass-fed beef, four chickens, tortillas, rice, beans (some dried and some canned), four packets of spaghetti, bananas, whatever other fruit was in season, milk, coffee, zucchini and other vegetables in season, flour, canned Hunt's pasta sauce (it's the cheapest at $0.99 a can instead of say, Ragu at $3), bread, a couple of jars of peanut butter, jelly, and two to three dozen eggs. I kept our kitchen stocked with oils, herbs, and sugar.

I would make all of our meals and snacks out of these ingredients all month and Bali would pick up milk and produce in the middle of the month. We also had enough money left for dog food and toiletries.

What I made from the daycare and food program reimbursement was around $2,000 per month. We paid everything easily. Our rent back then was $1,200 per month, but we had no Internet, no cable, only one car (owned free and clear), and absolutely no credit cards. Propane was the most expensive thing we had to pay for. I nursed, but we did buy disposable diapers and baby wipes.

When we moved to Walnut Grove to live on a fruit farm, we paid $1,300 per month in rent and had another baby on the way. We moved many counties over for a management position and wound up with a $10 per hour cashier job. But it was work and we liked our new house. It was the only house for rent when we needed to move. There was a big backyard for the dogs, and it was peaceful and lovely. Bali worked 70 hours weekly to bring home maybe $2,400 each month. Of that amount, $1,300 went to rent. I had $1,100 to work with. These are estimates, as this was years ago, and I don't have the sharpest memory. But it was close to these figures, give or take $10 or $100.

I only left the farm once a week to shop. This time, we had more affordable stores nearby – a Grocery Outlet, and a WinCo Foods. My childhood friend happened to live in the nearest town and was the one who introduced me to WinCo Foods. She said it was like a huge bin and candy store so I couldn't wait to see this. It was large and had a huge bulk bin section, and yes, they have quite the selection of bin candy. I did a full month's worth of shopping and I couldn't believe how small my total was at the register. This store would help us through lean times.

We found free wood and kindling and saved on energy with an attic whole house fan. We hung all the laundry on the clothesline outside and kept the lights off as much as possible.

I picked the fruit on the farm (with permission) and started baking bread and making laundry soap. I also attempted cloth diapers and did a little babysitting on the side.

The antenna picked up a lot of channels including PBS because we were so close to a TV satellite station. The local librarian taught me how to order materials from other libraries. Our entertainment came from lots of reading and watching old Westerns and '80s sitcoms.

When I first became a housewife, I was antsy. I was used to working two jobs, driving a lot, being busy with social events, having dinners out, being with friends, and walking Clyde for miles along the old logging roads and beach paths. I was busy all the time. Now, I was home. No car, no clocking in to a job at 8:30 a.m. each day, no chatting with friends at work all day, no projects of cleaning out the office supply closet or putting binders together, and no preparing classrooms for upcoming sessions. My house stayed clean because I didn't have children running about and making messes. I cooked from scratch but nothing like I do now. Scratch cooking was sautéing ground beef, pouring in a can of pasta sauce, and calling it dinner.

When Arjan came, I really had to be home. I had a Cesarean delivery and he nursed and slept all the time. I had to take it easy and it was too cold to walk around all the time. I was bored, so I tried to think up things I could do at home. I even took an online Spiritual Foundations class from the Center for Spiritual Living just to have something to do, but quickly learned that wasn't so easy to do. It required a lot of typing while "in class." Try nursing and typing. It doesn't work.

Arjan hated all things stroller, car seat, and MOBY wrap. He just wanted to be home and held in my arms. It made the simple act of taking a walk painful. I learned to bundle him up and time our walks around naptime. I would put him in the stroller, all wrapped up and covered, and start walking. The crying would quickly fade and turn into baby snores. I would often go to my old job where my former coworkers would excitedly greet us, and I would sit and drink green smoothies and visit with everyone during their 10-minute breaks.

My friend and her wife would have dinner parties and I only had to walk across the field to get to their house. They still worked at the school, so it was a social event. I loved that life. I so enjoyed living in a town that is only four miles long and wide, being able to walk from one end to the other. I had so many friends from my old job. We even belonged to the local Calvary Chapel church and had friends there, too. Bali knew everyone since he ran the Circle K for years. We had community, the ocean right in front of us, and the mountains and forest behind us. I could drive through a magical old forest to the small mountain town over the hill where I had also worked, been involved with the theater, and had more friends. There is nothing like loving where you live and being surrounded by friends.

But we had to move, and many of our close friends moved around the same time. Those small towns don't always have the jobs to support a family.

When we lived in Walnut Grove, there was nowhere to walk and I had no way to get to town on foot. I knew no one and Bali used the car from morning to late at night. I had no choice but to completely surrender to our home, motherhood, and being alone. My family and house became the great focal point.

It was the best thing for me. I became calm and was 100% focused on my babies and home. I cooked plenty for Bali, making sure that he had coffee and breakfast every morning, and a filling lunch and dinner for the rest of the day. I sat with my children and read quietly often. Sometimes we watched a silly show or movie on one of the local channels. I was addicted to Amish fiction, so it helped with my new quiet life.

The friend I previously mentioned, who told me about WinCo Foods, was such a blessing. I hadn't seen her since we were 15 years old. She and I had been new at school and quickly became friends. She then joined a group of other friends, one of whom was Betty, but I didn't quite fit in, so I went on to find my own group. She then moved a year later. She happened to live in the next town over and Betty had kept us apprised of each other's lives through gossip, so we sort of still knew each other.

She and her two young sons came out to visit us when we moved to the orchards in the summer and we became friends again. This time I was new to the area and she helped me so much. She was a housewife back then, so she had the time to visit once a week. She loved coming out there to the farm. Back then, it was filled with 600 acres of pear trees and shade trees that surrounded us. We would talk and have lunch together and play with Arjan. She and I made vats of laundry soap. We swapped money-saving ideas. Then, once a week I would visit her in town to shop and she would show me where all the good stores were. Sometimes we would go for lunch at Chick-fil-A.

Her boys were older, so I was given tubs of clothes in great condition and I didn't have to buy Arjan or Sam clothes for the next four to five years, thanks to her. I still have some summer and fall clothes from her youngest son. This was the first year I bought full wardrobes.

Eventually, some old friends came to visit, and some would stay with us for a few days. I loved having company, but we didn't have a lot to offer in the way of entertainment. I would cook up a storm, make and bake lots of delicious snacks, and order movies from the library as we had no video rental store. We would eat, talk, drink coffee, take drives in the country, and watch movies. Some friends had children, so we would help each other out with feeding, bathing, and playing.

Life was simple. Simple is good. Simple doesn't require much money. Simple brings deep meaning to time with friends, time with the spouse, and time with babies and children.

I even cooked simply back then. I can't remember looking up recipes or getting fancy. I used boxed brownie, cake, and cookie mixes. I used my *Dump Dinners* recipes that required a can, a pasta, a meat, a casserole dish, and 30 minutes. We ate peanut butter sandwiches for lunch often.

Then we moved to town. I had more money to work with and more time since we had a tiny house that only took 45 minutes to clean. I took the boys to the library and local parks all the time. We joined some homeschooling groups to get a feel for it. My friend was really far away now, and I think she started working so we never saw each other anymore. I only had two people visit me: one friend and my cousin's wife . . . once. They weren't as enchanted with our tiny house and crammed suburban neighborhood. But I had found a new passion in writing, and we loved walking all over the place and finding new places to hike, explore, and run around.

I had been frugal for years and now I spent the extra money on sliced bread, frozen lasagna, and some traveling to be with family and friends. You see, now we had a truck *and* the car, so I could run about during the day. I was alone often and had tired of being home. I visited family and friends in Marin, Truckee, Fort Bragg, and in Oregon. We had a lot of fun visiting people and if we wanted to be with friends and family we had to travel.

Getting the extra vehicle had its pros and cons. Connie Hultquist is right in saying that not having a car is a good thing. You don't run about all the time wasting gas and money. You stay home and tend to the house, save money, and find free ways to pass your time. When you don't have a car you just settle into your home. You have no option.

Now here we are in this lovely cottage, in the present. I still have the truck and we do have a lot more money at our disposal, but I have gone from one extreme to the other with being home all the time instead of being out and about and traveling often. I love this house. My focus is on nesting, learning to cook on many new levels – mainly a vegetarian and plant-based diet – and saving money so we can buy our dream house in our dream town.

As I write this, we have guests coming tomorrow and the next day. One of our guests, who lives in Oregon, has been a dear friend since we lived in Fort Bragg and worked at the same school together. She and I have stayed in touch and she has stuck by us no matter where we lived. I am excited that she will be visiting for the third time and staying all through the Thanksgiving holiday. Also, my friend from high school who kept me company during the Walnut Grove years will bring her family the day before Thanksgiving. It is now our families' tradition to share a Friendsgiving day each year. They live even farther now but will come for holidays and the boys' birthdays. I'm a pretty good cook now, so I can lure people with my food and homemade cakes.

In this town, we are starting to have community again. Bali knows all the locals from working at the station. People love him, even the big rednecks. We have a 20% Punjabi Indian population here, so we don't experience any prejudice. I know most of the neighbors on my street and have had many barbecues and dinners with them. I've attended my next-door neighbor's baby shower, and sent soup and fresh tomatoes over to my sick, elderly neighbor who lives across the street. I know what is going on with everyone. Some neighbors are kinder than others and that is normal.

But it is up the mountain where the boys attend classes at a charter and an outdoor school. I'm a co-op member at the health food store up there and am gaining many friends with children the same age as mine.

I would like to move up the mountain as it's all forest, and the forest calls me. The people there are more *my* people. I have two communities again and I haven't felt lonely once since moving here. I hope to never have to move somewhere far again.

So, I tuck money away all the time for this grand purchase. Right now, houses are insanely priced, but if we keep saving, there will be a time when the prices will drop again, and we will have a big chunk to put down on a mortgage loan.

We do a lot of 'no spends' seasons. Right now, with the holidays, it's not possible to do, but I can prepare. I've been hitting the stores, preparing for our guests and Thanksgiving celebrations. Every time I go, I stock up on great sales, so I have more than enough for my guests to eat all week, plus two big suppers, and some extra to stock my pantry well.

In December, I will have to order presents for the boys online, since we are limited to Walmart for toys here. I also bake a lot during this month, since I like to pass out tins of homemade cookies and candies to our neighbors, dentist, doctors, mail carriers, chiropractors, and whoever else I can't think of right now. I'm also doing a lot of baking for bake sales the kids' Earth school is having until the end of this school session. We also have a child in El Salvador who we sponsor, so I send extra to his village. We will buy a goat for a farmer through Heifer International and donate to Toys for Tots. It is the season for giving, after all.

After all the donations, our gifts to the children, Santa's gifts, and all the baking, we won't go broke, surprisingly. It's because I have that money sort of set aside, in my mind. It doesn't cost me that much because, first off, Christmas is for children. I only buy gifts for them; not for the family, friends, or even my husband or myself. I buy two gifts each for Arjan and Sam. One is the gift they pine over and dream about, usually under $50. The other is art supplies, and this year pajamas are added to the list since they have just outgrown theirs. It will total around $100 per child. To make the pot sweeter at Christmas, I will load up their stockings with toys, trinkets, and candy from Dollar Tree. I buy ornaments and little bags of dinosaurs and cars. I like to include those long, thick candy canes that I remember from my childhood. I will also buy three bags' worth of art supplies, toys, and candy canes for the children across the street.

Christmas baking is cheap. I usually make sugar cookies and frosting, Puppy Chow, Fudge, and Buckeye Balls. Maybe this year I'll make cinnamon candy, too. All I need is a lot of sugar and flour, some chocolate chips, canned milk, peanut butter, and Rice Chex cereal. I can stock up at WinCo Foods. It's all easy to make but does take a full day of devotion. My kitchen becomes a candy factory on this one day and I usually shove a Stouffer's frozen lasagna in the oven so everyone can eat servings of that all day. I couldn't do my daily cooking as well as all this baking. Perhaps I'll do the cinnamon candy separately on another day. I'll need a candy thermometer. You really must pay attention when doing hard candy. Still, it's all easy once you get the hang of it and people love homemade candy.

I don't send cards. People don't seem to be into them anymore. I could be wrong. Maybe I'll do that this year. I used to. I get packs of cards from the Humane Society and ASPCA because of the monthly donations I make. I also get those fantastic address labels and envelope seals. I used to send those out and get cards in return. I would hang the cards everywhere. I miss that. I have decluttered all my Christmas cards and must say that I regret doing that. Some things are meant to be saved, treasured, and hung each year to remind you of family and friends.

I would say that I can do Christmas for under $500 including gifts, cards, baking, bags of goodies for the neighborhood children, and a dinner on Christmas Eve and Christmas Day. It looks far more luxurious because we have the tree fully decorated with charming old decorations everywhere. We have Christmas music playing all day, and big candles in green and red. The whole house is a celebration of this season.

The last things I do for the season is hit the thrift store for their huge sale after Christmas, when all of their holiday items are 50% off. I find beautiful old decorations for the tree and hearth. Last year, Arjan and I found our new fake tree that is just gorgeous, as well as a box packed full of decorations and Christmas plates. So this year we don't need to buy anything, and we saved a good $75 on a real tree. However, I must admit that it's quite magical going to the lot after Thanksgiving, picking up a tree, and enjoying that fresh pine smell.

I have one more expense after Christmas, and that is preparing for fostering babies. I need a crib, mattress, blankets, cloth diapers, burp cloths, bottles, baby clothes, a tub, high chair, and who knows what else? It's been a few years. I will spend the next few months searching garage sales, although there aren't too many now that we're going into winter. Craigslist is a great way to buy loads of clothes at a low price as well as used cribs in good condition. And thrift stores are fantastic for baby clothes, blankets, books and toys.

I'm estimating that it will all cost a few hundred dollars to really be stocked and prepared to foster any child, from infant to toddler age.

I will get all this done before the end of December and try to stay within budget. Starting in the new year we will begin a 'no spend season.' I'm not sure how long it'll last, since emergencies pop up and life loves to throw you curveballs.

People love to debate over what a 'no spend' is. Ruth Soukup wrote *31 Days of Living Well and Spending Zero* and it is all about not spending anything for a month and breaking the habit of shopping mindlessly and eating out all the time. A month would be easy. You pay your bills and rent or mortgage ahead of time, fill the gas tanks and set aside an envelope with what you think you'll need for gas, and you eat from the pantry, freezer, and refrigerator for the rest of the month. Many people have full pantries because they shop all the time but then order takeout or go out to eat. They have food that is spoiling. Many people have enough food in their kitchen to last a month.

Now, if you are thinking of doing a season, a few months, or a year of 'no spend,' you will obviously be paying the rent or mortgage, the bills, commuting costs in either bus tickets or gas for the car. You will need groceries. But you could just pay for the basics and nothing else. When Bali and I do this, we have all our coffees, meals, and snacks at home. There is no going out to movies, dinner, shopping, or extras.

I would like to do a 'no spend' for our family budget for a few months starting in the new year. We can do it easily since we have plenty and my pantries are stocked.

I would like to write up a solid budget and foolproof it. If I know how much we need for the bills, gas, and mortgage, I will know exactly how much we can pay ourselves first. Another good way to set boundaries it to decide how much you truly need for groceries. This will include pet food and toiletries, as well as cleaning supplies.

Things have changed so much with our vegetarian diet. Now that I make my own soy milk and faux meats and buy in 25 lb and 50 lb bulk, I spend far, far less than I ever have on groceries. Having food in our garden and even being able to can and store some food from the summer vegetable garden has helped a lot.

I will set it at $500 and see how we do. I have a chart that gives figures on what the average cost of food is in the United States, from a thrifty plan all the way up to a liberal one. Even the low cost plan for a family of four was over $600 per month. Here is a link to their latest figures:

https://fns-prod.azureedge.net/sites/default/files/media/file/CostofFoodDec2019.pdf

I just think of it this way: what if you only had $500 for everything? You would do it. You would find sales, coupons, deals, and be very creative. So, in a way, if you want to save money and lower your spending you must set amounts and commit.

Paying ourselves has been life changing, literally. Bali and I don't bicker or argue over the budget. He is happy every month when he deposits his first paycheck into the savings account and sees it take another leap up. Our grocery budget is the only area that needs to be set up at a designated amount. What is left over must suffice for all the other bills, mortgage and gas. If we don't have enough for gas, we simply don't go anywhere. We are lucky in that our life is set up so that we don't have to travel. The kids are homeschooled. Bali can walk to work. I could save a tank of gas all month if I had to.

It's not hard to live on a small income if you make smart choices, purchase a house with a small mortgage, stay out of debt, and buy used cars paid for in cash. That is really all you have to do, and you can sleep well at night and enjoy a full life with many luxuries.

Chapter 12

My Past Writings to Inspire

Here are some handpicked blog posts that I wrote in 2019. I share my insights on managing a household, what I would do if we were very poor, how I make budgeting and cleaning simple for me, and how to stock the pantry on a small budget.

Brainless Budgeting and the Bliss in a Simple Life

I've been up with the roosters and the sound of the early morning train whistle in search of budgeting blogs. Actually, I was trying to find a particular blog I just loved by a single mother who lives quite simply. Instead, I found all the fancy budgeting websites. These sites are supposed to be about frugal living, but I have to disagree.

I'm going to sound critical and maybe even snarky here, but most of these sites, although very smart and creative, aren't what I need right now. They are shiny, trendy, and have "shops" where you can buy budget calendars and time schedulers, cute money envelopes, and many other colorful baubles and stickers to keep you on track.

I do have a planner that I love, but I only use a quarter of it. I tried stickers and had a field day reconnecting with the child in me who once had a fabulous sticker book. I stickered that calendar right up, but despite the cute stickers with a pink washer or that adorable loaf of bread, I didn't always follow through with those scheduled baking days or laundry days. Some days I did, but others, not so much.

I don't do well with spreadsheets. They remind me of the time when I attempted a very corporate job and detested it so much that I walked out after a month of gray, grueling days of inputting numbers.

An old calendar that the Humane Society sends me annually works just fine. A notebook from Dollar Tree is perfect for a budget. After all, you only need to write it out on one sheet of paper. Old envelopes from paper bills work perfectly as money envelopes. Pencils, calculators, and highlighters are all great for writing out all the ways you won't be spending money this month. Or the next, next, and next.

Frugal blogs that sell sparkly stuff to help you save money are silly. Fun, perhaps, but when you are in the trenches and bleeding money, a spreadsheet ain't going to save the day.

What *will* save the day is simply to stop all spending . . . full stop! Don't leave the house, don't order anything online, just stop moving and thinking for a bit. Then get some good old-fashioned advice. *The Complete Tightwad Gazette* by Amy Dacyczyn is old school but those old school gals knew a thing or few hundred about saving some big-time cash.

Here is a plan, Phase 1:

- Stop spending. You pay the rent/mortgage, the groceries and utilities, and gas for the vehicle to get to work and/or school. If you ride the bus, you set aside your bus fare.
- Cut the grocery bill in half. No dining out. No coffee at Starbucks. No takeout or take in or take about! You eat, snack, and make lattes at home. You make food in your kitchen that you take to work/school.
- You write out a budget and stick to it.
- Cut out extras. Cable is so unnecessary in this day and age. Cancel the gym membership (I'm having issues with this). You can walk outside for free (line from the movie *Brittany Runs a Marathon*).
- Get a job close to home.
- Find cheaper housing.
- Walk to work.

Then, once you have mastered all this over the next few to six months, you go on to Phase 2:

- Reduce utilities and learn about the Go Green Movement. Use less water, go solar, etc.
- Drink ice water instead of soda. Your intestines and your wallet will thank you.
- Learn to cook from scratch.
- Bake your own breads, cakes, and muffins. Have your own bakery at home.
- Learn to use what you have. I highly doubt that you need to make a trip to Dollar Tree. You have whatever it is in a drawer, closet, or garage. If you have an attic or storage unit, it's probably in there.
- Get rid of the storage unit.
- Find frugal friends.
- Learn the joys of potlucks and dinner parties at home instead of $200 dinners out.

Easy Ways to Manage the Home & Cooking for the Single and Working Parent

I am not a working parent. Well, yes, I am. But I work from home and on my terms. I rise naturally and not with an alarm; I work as I please and when I feel moved to create. I write and have a YouTube channel that generates enough money to afford organic food and to be able to say that I work.

But for a working parent or a single parent, work is an alarm, having to rise unnaturally and oftentimes in the dark. There may be a long commute and having to work for someone else, doing what they want you to do. Not only that, but there are children to get to school and pick up hours later, then homework, baths, and bedtime. It's too much.

Weekends are probably the only time that this family has to clean, do laundry, and shop for groceries.

I've been thinking about this a lot, trying to figure out ways for the working and/or single parent to manage the household and cooking more efficiently, so that they have more time to play and rest.

We know that cooking from scratch is the healthiest and most cost-effective way to go. But if you work and commute all the time, this can be a downright pain in the rear. A clean and tidy house might be doable since no one is home to mess it up during the day.

I have a big planner that I buy from JOANN. In it, I can make To Do lists and schedule everything. And I do, in colored pens, and with highlighters. I decorate this book from top to bottom and love it because it is a colorful visual aid to getting and keeping me organized and on schedule. I used to schedule my cleaning days, baking days, laundry days, write down appointments, and birthdays. I'm not into calendars or reminders on the cell phone. Phones get deleted, stolen, and lost. There is something about a book that you touch and look at in full that I love. I keep it right next to my laptop. I used to even keep track of how many words I would write each day.

This all may sound rigid, but it wasn't. In fact, it was very flexible, and I turned it into my daily rituals. One day would be a baking day and I had a routine and ritual for that day. Even laundry day had its rituals, like when I had afternoon tea and watched a sitcom on TV, guilt-free, because I was "folding laundry."

As I've said before, I don't always stick to this schedule. But I may go back to it because it felt good. It was organized, so I didn't have to think. I would look at the book and know what my day and week were looking like.

I also have a big blue binder filled with lined paper, both of which were purchased at a thrift store. In this binder, I do all my kitchen management. I schedule weeks' worth of meals and make grocery lists. I have a section for my pantry inventory and make a list of what to buy. I also copy recipes that I use often or find in cookbooks from the library. I no longer buy cookbooks as they just collect dust.

The envelope system is also a great way to not overspend. At the beginning of the month, I pay all the bills and mortgage and then get cash for a grocery envelope and whatever else. I try to not use cards these days. It's too easy to swipe them and mindlessly spend yourself into trouble at the bank. With cash envelopes, you're aware of what you have for the month and you will become very clever in the grocery store. You will find ways to make that envelope last and last, especially after a month or two of winding up short at the end of the month. Touching money makes you think.

It may sound silly, but calendars and notebooks in vibrant colors and cash that you can touch make all the difference. We are in such a digital age that we tap away frantically at our cell phones and have them managing everything for us. But the old-fashioned ways work well because you must slow down, become present, and touch and see pages; you write with pens and pencils, calculate and think. When I do this, I must sit down with my colored pens and calendar and think about my month, setting it up in my mind.

Unless you love shopping, the other way to really save time and money is to build an incredible pantry. Do your shopping once a month and each time, build it in layers until you have everything and anything you need to cook meals, bake cakes for birthdays or cookies for the bake sale; even make your own cleaners, laundry detergent, homemade beauty products, shampoos, and playdough for the kids. You could turn it into your own personal store and shop from it daily. Almost anything you can think of for the home can be made from scratch.

Bulk cooking and meal prepping once a week can be fun and make a huge difference. If you have freezer space, you could take a weekend to cook large amounts of food to freeze and have ready for the whole month. Or you could take just one day a week to prep food for the work week. Another trick is to always cook an extra batch to freeze. Make two lasagnas and freeze one. Make two or three enchilada casseroles and freeze the extra. It builds up, and then you have meals for when you are too tired.

Master one-pot dishes, especially the slow cooker. That slow cooker is amazing because you can throw things in there and leave for the whole day, return home at night, and you have dinner ready. I know that the Instant Pot is all the rage these days, but I would rather prep in the morning and come home to a hot meal. A bread maker is also a magical little gadget. You can have fresh, homemade bread when you come home from work or set the timer so that it's fresh in the morning. Set the coffee timer as well and you will awaken to the smells of freshly baked bread and brewing coffee. What a dream!

As for cleaning, do a hardcore, deep clean once a month and then light clean weekly. If the children are old enough, have them help with the chores. It's a community, and children need to contribute. They need to learn how to cook and clean so that when they get out into the world, they can create cozy homes and tend to themselves and their families.

The biggest way to simplify cleaning is to be decluttered and organized. Everything must have its place. Clean out the drawers and downsize the closets. Get rid of the extra stuff. A good purging will reduce cleaning by 25% to 50%. It's easy to keep the house nice and tidy when you don't have clutter. I watch videos to get ideas or get motivated. I'm deep in a decluttering session at the moment. I sort of feel like the more I declutter the more I find. The mind and body crave that space, to have things clean, tidy, and orderly. As a bonus, think of all the hours upon hours you save by NOT looking for missing socks or shirts.

Paying Off a Mortgage Within Five Years and How to Build Big Savings Fast

Choices. I said something real smart the other day. It was something along the lines of, "Our choices today make up our harvest tomorrow." Brilliant! Someone may have already said this and I'm copyrighting. We have all heard this sort of saying about how today's choices are tomorrow's . . . or yesterday's choices are today's something or other.

One of our top priorities is to pay off our mortgage as fast as we can. I'm really pissed off after Bali pointed out that we have paid $24,000 on our mortgage in the last two years and we only made a tiny $5,000 dent on the balance! I knew that the bank was taking some interest and that it was going to take some time to pay the mortgage off, but it's not until you really read that monthly mortgage statement that you begin to understand just what a huge chunk the bank takes and how little goes to the principal. Then you add things up after a few years and that is when you slam your hand down on your lovely thrifted table and yell, "The injustice of this all!"

I recently spoke with a new friend from my YouTube community about this, and she greatly inspired me with a story she shared about how she paid off her mortgage within five years. The woman is a single foster parent of six adopted children. One of her children was dealing with a major illness at the time and she had taken out a loan to pay huge medical bills, but still managed to pay her mortgage off, despite all her obstacles. Now, I didn't ask her what the beginning balance was, but who cares? She did it, and so can we.

In this time and age of debt and consumerism along with an impending recession lurking in the shadows, it seems prudent to have a mortgage-free house. I see the housing market still climbing in some areas, stalling in some, and only declining in areas where the houses are already in the absurd millions or so. I see rent doubling and hear the news about tenants complaining about increases and how they have to move out of their apartments that have been their homes for years. And it's all because the greedy landlord is wanting a piece of the high rent pie.

I'm very grateful to have a house. I'll feel more solid and we will live even more simply once it's mortgage-free.

Here is an inspirational video about a woman who paid off her house in only three years: https://www.youtube.com/watch?v=i2dB_4x2iOE

You know what else makes you feel safe when you wake in the middle of the night? Having a substantial savings. I'd say at least six months' worth. Then you know that if something happens, as they always do, you can get by for six months.

But how, you ask? Dave Ramsey is really the person to go to but since I've listened to him and checked out his book *The Total Money Makeover* twice, I'll share what I know.

First, you go here:

https://www.daveramsey.com/mortgage-calculator

You type in your mortgage, enter $0 down payment, and your current interest rate. Click on the 15-year mortgage. It will give you a new mortgage payment. It includes taxes, insurance and MIP (mortgage insurance premium). If you don't have MIP, just subtract that. Unfortunately, we still have it.

That will be the new monthly payment.

If you want to shorten this even more, you pay an extra payment each quarter. When income tax refunds come, you apply these as well. Every time you have any extra money you throw it at your mortgage. But make sure those loan people know that extra payments go toward the principal only.

Now, if you want to save fast and big, try the following:

Take that income tax refund and deposit it in a separate bank, preferably a local credit union, as they tend to *not* nickel and dime you. You then work out a budget and figure out how much you can save each month. A good amount to start with is 10%. Set a goal to save and deposit as large a chunk as possible and commit.

The next trick is to put the money in the savings account the first of every month. You can also have your bank automatically deposit a set amount at the beginning of each month. Whatever works best for you is what you do.

We found that what works best for us is to have an account in a separate bank and deposit the first paycheck of the month into it. The second paycheck pays our mortgage two weeks early, and then we live off any royalties I bring in from my books and YouTube. We live on around $2,000 a month by choice because we committed to saving $1,000 a month. Sometimes it's less than $2,000 and the account gets overdrawn a bit or we get creative with the lentils and barley, but we stay on course no matter how tempting a grocery haul or thrift store shopping spree may be.

We make do or do without, just like our grandparents during the Great Depression! Use it up, wear it out, make do, or do without!

Tonight, I made the last of our ground beef into a spaghetti sauce and I threw in extra sauce to stretch it for two days' worth of meals. I had to put an old thrift store lamp out by the garbage as it was worn out, but I didn't even think about getting another. I just rotated the lamps in the house to make up for the missing light.

Those are tiny things but they add up. I also ground some coffee beans in the blender, as I won't buy a coffee grinder. It worked great, by the way. I baked bread in the bread maker for tomorrow's toast and sandwiches. We grew sprouts on the windowsill and simmered a pot of black beans.

I've stocked my pantry well so I'm only shopping for $50 worth of groceries every seven to ten days. I find that I only need a few items such as potatoes, onions, soy milk, and bananas to make many tasty meals with the assorted beans, lentils, and grains we already have. I've learned to make cool things like quinoa bread, and that I can use oat flour when I run out of all-purpose flour.

When there is extra money, or I do get to go on a tiny grocery shopping spree, it is almost as exciting as a trip to Disneyland . . . almost. When I'm blessed with a gift card or a bag of hand-me-downs, I am thrilled beyond thrilled. Little things that are often taken for granted mean so much now.

It's all a game and you can be miserable or really enjoy it and thrive as you successfully beat the system and cheat the bank. In the end, you will be so proud of what you have accomplished, and when others are still struggling to pay a huge mortgage, you will be at Goodwill having that shopping spree you waited five years to have.

My Job as a House Manager

I love waiting in dental and doctors' offices. I am the one person who has no problem when the staff are running late (if I have no children, that is). I bring a book and enjoy that quiet time, amen!

The other day I waited my turn for a teeth cleaning and enjoyed some time reading *Introduction to Home Economics: Gentle Instruction to Find Joy in Christian Homemaking* by Mrs. Sharon White. The entry was about a homemaker's worth in dollars. We have read many articles on this and I have even discussed this in my videos before.

We add up the salary of a driver, cook, maid, secretary, teacher, butler, nanny, etc. We calculate what it would cost to pay a gardener to mow the lawns, the amount to pay a dog walker, the costs of daycare, and a part-time house cleaner. Don't forget to add up takeout, delivery, restaurants, Starbucks, and the deli down the block from work.

But I've got a new spin on this old topic. When others ask you what you do all day, or tell you to get a job, put the kids in school, and get on with it (as if you may be lazing in fields of clover and letting the children run wild in the streets while others are actually being productive members of society), you tell them that you are a house manager and your boss would become hysterical at the loss of one of his (or her) most valuable employees.

After all, you are running that small world your family lives in, which you call "home."

No need to get up in arms. As Jesus said, "Forgive them for they know not what they do." Right? I've had rude people come on my YouTube channel and say to me that I need to put my children in school and go back to work. Guess what I do with those people? I report them as either hate speech or harassment. Yessir! I ain't messin' around, people!

Now, let's get this straight. I'm no Martha Stewart or queen of organization and I certainly can't hold a candle to the home cooks out there making fancy jellies and stews, but I work on it daily.

I get lazy. I buy and bake premade foods. My house is shameful at times. I can't fold worth a darn, even with all the Marie Kondo shows on how to fold. My skill set makes my friends' eyes roll. It makes them tell me it's too painful to watch.

Deep cleaning is a new thing for me. I have been known to do chores in my pjs. In fact, I find them quite suitable for daywear (only at home though). Not much about my home is Instagram worthy and few of my ideas are Pinterest ready.

Despite a list of faults and shortcomings, I am a wonderful mother and homemaker most of the time (a good portion of the time...frequently)!

I am the House Manager! It's the new title I gave myself today after a few days of pondering this whole topic. I should be earning a good and solid $60,000 a year with benefits, paid holidays and vacations, weekends off, plus much more.

We know this is not realistic, so I will forgo weekends and take my work with me (a.k.a. family) on holidays and vacations. However, I insist on time off in the form of a movie alone in a dark theater with Milk Duds and delicious, buttery popcorn, especially when the next Star Wars movie comes out. This is non-negotiable.

I will also add to the list (since I don't get evenings or nights off) that a gym membership at my favorite racquet club is added as well as some extra cash now and then for thrifting.

Oh, alright! Forget the $60,000 annual salary, but the gym membership, movie night and extra cash now and then are non-negotiable! Period!

Now that I've at least evaluated my worth, let's see what I offer, shall we?

I manage the house, as the title suggests. This includes work in the following areas: administrative, maintenance, cleaning, organization, and financial affairs. I make appointments and make sure subjects arrive at those appointments, be they medical, dental, chiropractic, and so on. I sign children up for independent study and an outdoor forest school. I retrieve, complete, and submit necessary paperwork and plan out classes, schedules, curriculum, and order proper materials. There is also homeschooling where I'm responsible for the education and development of two humans so that when they go out into the world, they are prepared on many levels. It is my duty to be sure that they are well-mannered, compassionate, and become valuable community members.

As for the housework, there is daily cleaning, weekly all-over cleaning, seasonal deep cleaning, and the big chores I save for yearly self-torture. There are rooms that need organizing of clothes, kitchen tools, bathroom supplies, as well as gadget control. Cleaning solutions need to be made or purchased. Sometimes repairs and maintenance need to be scheduled with professionals. I make those appointments and make sure that things are done in a timely manner.

There are kitchen gardens, fruit, nut, and citrus trees that need planting, weeding, harvesting, and feeding. There is watering, mowing, and pruning. There are seasonal schedules to be followed. A lot of research goes into this as I'm new to the gardeners' side of things.

The kitchen is where I spend a lot of my work hours. There are menus to look up and plan, shopping to keep pantries full, and inventory to manage. I have a strict budget and have found ways to make it stretch by planting my own organic food. I am also learning the craft of canning and drying food. Waste is down to almost nothing due to effective waste management by only buying what's needed, composting scraps, and either freezing, drying, or preserving what is near expiration. Most food is made from scratch so there are recipes to look up and new dishes to learn to cook all the time.

I am the house baker. There is no rising early to bake the loaves of the day. However, there is almost daily work required in the form of baking loaves of bread, crackers, and muffins. I make homemade tortillas. Some days there are even cakes to mix, rise, knead, and bake.

Then we have the finances. This one requires the writing up of budgets, strict buckling down, and using envelopes and restraint. Utilities and resources must be used wisely to keep the costs down. A savings must be built through cutting out excessive needs/wants and making do with what is at hand. Sometimes extensive research and investigation are needed to reduce interest rates on the house mortgage or new ideas incorporated such as solar panels and a clothesline. The bills must be paid in a timely manner and it is important that the funds are available at these times. Future retirement and education are also an investment to be worked toward so thrift and frugality are a must on all levels of running the home and tending to the family.

There are smaller jobs of baths for not just the children, but the dogs, as well. The trash bins must be taken out on garbage night.

Thought we were done? Oh no, Dear Reader, we have a bit to go yet. The duties of a House Manager are many.

There is the family wardrobe. This includes knowing everyone's sizes, searching in thrift stores, garage sales, and online at discount stores. It means accepting hand-me-downs with gratitude. There is the washing and organizing of all clothes. The storing of clothes that are not yet the right size or not for the season at hand. There are stains to wash out by hand, holes to be mended, and the occasional ironing. Though the washer kindly washes the clothes, at times, things need special washing in the sink or soaking in special solutions. In the warm seasons, clothes are hung outside on the garden clothesline. It is important that the family has the proper clothes for the weather, so inventory is key here. There is ordering the raincoats, snow boots, or whatever else is needed to keep everyone warm or well-ventilated.

Exercise is important. Children need park time, swimming time, nature hikes, and trips to the beach. The sun provides vitamin D, the fresh air cleans their lungs. My husband, Bali, does need some coaxing in this department at times, but it is important that the House Manager works out daily to keep her mood cheerful and her body strong for all the tasks and chores.

The house is to be made into a home and work is required to make it charming and cozy. This means more research in magazines, websites, and vlogs. Time and thought must be put into the decorating, and a small budget is to be adhered to. A small budget means many visits to browse the local hospice, thrift, or street yard sale for little treasures to fill the home with comfort and color.

Nutrition is important. Much studying and research must be done when it comes to illnesses, vaccines, organic food, and how to feed the family in a way that will reduce sickness, disease, and future doctor bills. This is where growing and preserving food comes in. Knowledge of vitamins and how to cook delicious and nutritious foods that everyone will eat and enjoy is crucial.

The pets also need care, healthy food, and veterinary appointments. Sometimes it's necessary to actually cook dog food from scratch or boil bone broth to ensure they stay healthy or recover from a mild doggy ailment.

Car maintenance, exercising the dogs, and heavy digging in the garden is left up to the mister of the house, along with working outside our humble abode to bring home the money I will then divide, save, and pay bills with.

Bali is the provider and protector. He is kind in doing all those small and large chores I set aside for him because the chores are either too strenuous, or have to do with cars, and that is far beyond my job knowledge.

I'm also the house nurse and counselor. You wouldn't think that a 5-year-old and a 7-year-old would need therapy, but those two are full of tiny world drama over stolen dinosaurs, a misplaced toy, or some little person insult that provokes wrath. I wipe many tears and have to mediate many arguments and help a little person navigate through feelings about life, the world, and others. I do this daily.

I have spent many nights up with sick ones and had to fuel myself with espressos to get through a 24-hour shift with little to no sleep. It comes with the territory.

I am also the house entertainment and activity director. I make sure we all have fun. I plan events to farms for apple picking during the fall, and I gather friends for Thanksgiving feasts. I plan a full month of Christmas celebrations that include baking, decorating, and singing carols. Outside of holidays, we have the seasonal crafts and celebrations. In the summer, we swim and hike. We take library trips weekly, play at the park, and meet friends for scheduled playdates. This doesn't happen all the time but it has to be planned and kept up. When I'm tired, I settle for reading books to the children, putting on music, and encouraging them to play on their own outside.

The last thing I can think of that is a major duty is the decluttering, organizing, and care of our household items. This requires going through cupboards, closets, and drawers often to keep things updated and clean. Keeping the clutter cleared helps in keeping an orderly house.

I believe that I've covered all my tasks. I'm not sure; I will probably think of a few more in the middle of the night but the point has been made.

Show your mother-in-law, sister, or neighbor this article when they suggest you go to "work" or get a "real job." Show this to your friend or spouse when they ask "What do you do all day?" Then, if it's a spouse, leave for the week on a family emergency (at the beach preferably) and let them figure out what to "do all day."

*Keeping Your Home Clean, Tidy, and Fresh Without Losing Your S****

I've been obsessed with finding the perfect cleaning routine. One that will change the way I housekeep forever, that will change my life, my family's life, and will give me more time to do the things that I love! I want a super clean, sparkly, and fresh home; the kind that makes you want to take a deep breath and inhale that lemony scent as you put your arms out and spin.

But that's not what I have right now. Instead, I have cobwebs that I notice when I don't have a broom nearby. I have filthy baseboards that I notice when in the middle of another duty, and dead flies on my windowsill that have been there since last summer. You get the point.

I watch all these damn FlyLady videos with her team showing us how to clean, but they don't. She doesn't. They sit there and drone on about it and I just want to see this formula at work. I want to see these ladies busting their humps. I watched five videos and still only have a morning and nighttime routine and the classic old timer trick that I've used for years.

I have to say, since I started faithfully going back to my routines, it's much easier to keep up. But where are the heavy duty details? Where is the vlog of FlyLady scrubbing baseboards on her knees?

I read an article about 1950s housewives' routines. They cleaned for three hours in the morning. That could really get you caught up and be more than enough time to bang out another project like reupholstering a chair or building a shed out back.

There is another way to go to get super organized for the whole year. Pam Young and Peggy Jones wrote a book called *Sidetracked Home Executives: From Pigpen to Paradise.* This method involves index cards. I'm not interested, but Granny loves this system and has set up two family members on it. She swears by it. It just sounds like there are a lot of cards involved.

I did receive a used planner and at first, just shoved it in a drawer, but I have since brought it out. With colorful pens and Wite-Out, I made a monthly schedule. I have an activity on each day of the week.

It seems that people are getting as complicated and obsessed with scheduling housework as they are with these fad diets. "Oh, I only eat meat now. I'm on a keto diet." "Yes, and I only mop on Tuesdays. It's my new FlyLady routine." This is only my impression. I'm no fan of the keto diet nor am I enamored with the FlyLady or S.H.E. (Sidetracked Home Executives) methods. Too much thinking – and work!

I feel like acting out.

I'll tell you what works for me: getting a housecleaning lady. Yes, that is the solution, but we are on a mission to save money and that doesn't seem to be in the budget these days.

So, I have a simple routine. I have the calendar book to keep me on track and not forget things like appointments with Arjan's homeschool teacher. I have a nightly routine that really makes my mornings pleasant because the kitchen is clean and tidy, the house is tidy, and the table is washed. Then I have a quick morning routine of making beds, brewing coffee, cooking breakfast, and checking my schedule for the day. This is a FlyLady thing. But she suggests dressing and putting on your shoes, and that irks me as shoes are the filthiest things you could wear in your home. We don't wear shoes in our home.

Every day, I take an hour to do some housecleaning. I like to set a timer and brew coffee. An hour a day becomes a lot as you catch up. I have other things I do such as clean the bathroom when the boys are bathing, or wash dishes as I wait for dinner to cook. To keep our home smelling good, I turn on my scented wax warmer now and then or I'll simmer cinnamon and cloves in a few cups of water on the stove's back burner.

Then there is shopping and cooking. I've decided to do one big shop for the month and then one in the middle of the month for some fresh produce and soy milk. I've also incorporated one day of meal prepping that I do every Sunday. This will involve making one month's worth of menus.

Obsessing about cleaning and having to shop and cook constantly is what wears down the homemaker. Making it easy and streamlined will change your life and free it up for hiking, gardening, writing a hit novel, and enjoying the children.

Here are some food prepping vlogs that inspired and helped me so much. One is for all types of food and one is more vegan. You will love them both.

https://www.youtube.com/watch?v=3VgtQjO_jK8&t=495s

https://www.youtube.com/watch?v=hpx2fh-RofU

Quick Way to Set Up a Pantry For Scratch Cooking

Frugal living is living below your means. It is exchanging one expense for another that might create a higher quality of life, not getting rid of all the fun things in life. It is learning the craft of living simply in order to have more of what makes life truly delicious and luxurious.

One way to save a huge amount of your monthly income is to learn to shop and cook differently. I recently uploaded a vlog about jumpstarting frugality. It is about extreme ways to start living below your means. This topic goes with it perfectly.

I love working from cookbooks that help you build your pantry and show you how to make everything under the sun using simple ingredients. I have found that *Dining On A Dime*, *Make-A-Mix Cookery*, *Dump Dinners*, and *Dump Desserts* (all referenced above) do exactly that.

After reading and working from these books, I have made a list of absolute must-haves to stock a proper pantry that will provide you with all the basics for scratch cooking.

- 25 lbs to 50 lbs of all-purpose flour
- 25 lbs of wheat flour
- 50 lbs of pinto beans
- 25 lbs of rice (white or brown)
- 20 bags of assorted pasta (spaghetti, macaroni, egg noodles, bow tie, etc.)
- 50 lbs of potatoes (russets are the cheapest)
- 20 lbs of onions (we prefer red)
- Large box or bag of powdered milk
- 20 large bags of frozen and mixed vegetables
- 25 lb bag of oats

- Huge jars of peanut butter
- 10 cans of water-packed tuna
- 10 lb bag of sugar
- 8 large cans of tomato sauce
- 1 to 2 lbs of raisins
- 20 lb bag of coffee (of course)
- A large container of powdered creamer

Seasonings (I purchase most of my seasonings from the bulk section at WinCo Foods):

- A gallon of oil (a healthy one, preferably)
- 2 or more lbs of salt
- 1/2 lb of granulated onion (I prefer the flavor much more than the powdered)
- 1/2 lb of granulated garlic
- 1/2 cup of Italian seasoning
- 1/2 cup dried thyme
- 1/2 cup dried basil
- 1/2 cup dried parsley
- 1/2 cup dried rosemary

Extra bulk seasonings to make dishes from scratch:

- 1 lb or more of cheese powder mix
- 1 lb of powdered peanut butter
- 1/2 cup chicken flavor powder

With these foods, you can make all your own crackers, cakes, bread, tortillas, fried potatoes and onions, mashed potatoes, casseroles, macaroni and cheese, bean dishes, burritos, soups, hot cereals, and more.

This is just a big and quick pantry starter list, but if you add to it each month with extra money from your grocery envelope, you will have nutritious and filling meals that taste delicious and down-home.

Once you have the basics, you can start adding:

- Big bags of corn tortillas for homemade chips and tacos.
- Large boxes of Krusteaz cornbread and pancake mixes. I love these as they only require water, and at the end of the month, you don't always have the oil, eggs, or milk that other mixes call for.
- Canned chili, beans (kidney, pinto, black, cannellini, garbanzo) and vegetables (all purchased on sale).
- Anything that your family likes, is on sale, and can be added to stretch a meal.
- Popcorn (don't forget that!)

Produce:

- Bananas (always very inexpensive)
- Any produce in season
- Large bags of carrots
- Celery
- Fruits and vegetables packaged in large bags as opposed to loose. For example, loose oranges will usually cost more than a 10 lb bag of oranges.

Condiments:

- Pickles
- Mayonnaise

- Mustard
- Ketchup

Some people go to food banks at the end of the day or month to ask for what they are about to throw out. This way, you are not taking from anyone in need, but saving food from the garbage. You can preserve and dehydrate the food quickly before it truly spoils.

If you need to save money, learn to live on less than you earn. If you are in debt, it is an absolute must to pay it off as quickly as possible. You can use your creative powers and become very industrious about foraging food, both inside and out of the city or town that you live in.

But always, always have fun! Make it into a game and learn the craft.

Enjoying My Days of Cleaning, Gardening, and Being Creative with a Reduced Budget

Ah, summertime. To us, summertime means a bounty of delicious produce and lots of swimming in any body of water that we come across. This year, summer is all about my two big kitchen gardens, creating some fun for the boys, and saving money.

It's also a time of changing my patterns of working too much and learning to slow down, become present, meditate during chores, and allowing my creative side to flourish.

I get so much satisfaction by decorating my home with little odds and ends I'm finding in closets and in the garage, and harvesting organic food from our gardens.

We are cutting costs, so I'm giving up my beloved health club membership, and I admit that it's caused some sadness since it gives the boys and I such joy. But then we traveled to a forest park with our friends the other day and enjoyed the lush forest as we swam in clear, clean water. I would choose that over the gym or public pool any day. As a bonus, it was free. God's beauty is free! Not only that, but when we swim in the gym pool outside, the boys get sick often because it is a festering pool of bacteria (the doctor's words, not mine). Something for me to ponder, right?

I've been moving shade umbrellas around in the yards, finding and picking up free truckloads of mulch, and learning new recipes. Dishes are being left in the sink. Although I do clean up the kitchen, wipe down counters, and sweep, I fill the sink with soapy water and let the dishes sit for a later hour. We have implemented a movie hour in the afternoon, after chores and free play. It's a quiet time to enjoy a movie, or I'll read a book aloud while Arjan creates his art.

I'm sewing up everything these days. I haven't attempted the quilt since the first time I couldn't figure out how to cut out the odd and complicated patterns, but I'm sewing up holes in my decorative pillows, stretch pants, and whatever else I can find. I mended two of my favorite stretch capri pants instead of throwing them out, saving myself $24.

Because I *am* home, I find free things on Craigslist, or I'm offered free items that others are decluttering, and I can go fetch a truckload during the day. I can't even begin to list the gifts I've dragged home for homesteading and gardening.

Since doing the last big house purge, I've created a smaller wardrobe from what survived the overhaul and I'm finding all these great things that were hidden under the junk. I decorated my sofa with my great-grandmother's lace tablecloth and found hair dye and nail polish from a year ago. I had a beauty spa day and now sport a blonde hairdo and purple toenails.

My mornings are busy with chores, writing, cooking, and talking with the boys. We play music and they read and create art. Since summer began, Arjan has ordered tons of books from the library, filling his days with reading fun books about mysteries and facts and learning how to draw dinosaurs. His reading and art skills have flourished. Sam is more into movies and fighting imaginary zombies.

In the afternoons, I like to make a delicious coffee drink with my new milk frother that I can't get enough of, and after a bit of sitting and reading quietly with the boys and a movie, I go on to cook supper before Bali gets home. Or I might go do some work in the garden, harvesting food or planting and watering.

Evenings are for prepping the stovetop percolator for my morning brew, washing up the last of the dishes, washing my face (which feels so good after a long day), brushing teeth, and relaxing with our favorite sitcoms while lying in the cozy family bed.

I go to bed tired from a busy day, but feeling accomplished. I rise (sometimes still tired) looking forward to a good cup of coffee and a productive morning ahead.

Sometimes when I work in the kitchen, I attach small speakers to my Chromebook and listen to Louise Hay or Dr. Joe Dispenza talk about healing our thoughts and minds to have a fuller and happier life. I love learning and working on myself as I go about washing and cleaning my home. I feel better for it afterwards.

It isn't always easy to do long 'no-spend' periods or to get up to do all the housework and cooking all over again. Cooking mostly from scratch can be like running a small restaurant.

That is why it is important to slow down, clear the calendar, and just be present in each task. Play with your house, decorate with what you have, purge, and scrub. Play with the children, watch afternoon movies for a nice break in the days' toils. Teach the children how to do chores so they can be helpful. Have them clean up after themselves. Learn as many easy meals as possible. Even pancakes can be healthy. We used to make honey wheat pancakes with fresh bananas, nuts, maple syrup, and even flax bran. Learn new skills to freshen up the job description and challenge yourself.

I watched a YouTube video on how to make a wedding cake and I want to try it sometime. I'm going to attempt the quilt again but use squares instead of patterns. Canning season will be here soon and that will keep me busy.

Don't do too much because it never ends, so the thinking that "I'll bust my bum today and rest tomorrow" doesn't happen. Do the basics and maybe a little extra project a day. An example would be to do the dishes, make the bed, sweep the kitchen, and maybe organize the pantry.

Don't try to be like other homemakers. Be you. Find what works for you. Find your cleaning and cooking styles and go for it. Don't try to reach perfection or it will send you to the loony bin. Do try to find fun and happiness in your work. Embrace it, relax into it, brew some coffee, and turn up the music.

Living on a Reduced Income and a 'No-Spend' Summer

We've created some changes in the last few days. The first big change was kindly asking my husband to quit his second job. The other changes had to come after that big executive decision. If a business (aka household) needs to cut costs, then they must come up with ways to reduce costs in the business and without sacrificing quality – if they are a smart business.

I made the decision to eliminate the second job because, upon careful observation of my husband's behavior, I decided that all this work was not good. I'm no psychologist but the man used to be pleasant and now he sleeps everywhere he lands, is very grumpy, and complains too often. *I'm* the official nag; he's stealing my thunder, here. Then, when I showed him videos of the boys and it was meant for amusement but only brought forth a sad face . . . well, I really felt that his days of long hours should be halted immediately.

We have a project in mind and we need money for it, so if he isn't going to have the extra job for building the savings, then we will have to use my royalties for it. That means we will go back to living on ONE. SMALL. INCOME. Drat.

We are a family of four living in Northern California. Life costs here. But we can do it on $2,300 per month (because that is our monthly income). I wrote out the budget in full detail, and if we cut out the health club when our membership expires in August, we can pay our mortgage and all the bills for under $1,600 a month. This does not include groceries and gas. However, it does leave us over $700 for groceries and gas.

How can we live on so little and with a mortgage? Well, some of you know what I'm gonna say. Cue the singsong voice: Buy a cheap fixer-upper and you'll never stress about the mortgage.

We only have two luxuries and those are the health club and Netflix. I will miss the health club, but Netflix is just meh. Crackle, GoStream, Vudu, and YouTube replace it just fine. I will admit that Amazon Prime has about four movies I'm dying to see, though.

The health club has pools, saunas, hot tubs, Kids Club, and so much more. I feel a bit depressed about this, but I remind myself that it's temporary. We can walk everywhere, save on gas, *and* exercise. I have exercise equipment in the garage and in the living room and you can get so much on YouTube. I even found The Firm workouts today!

As for groceries, I refuse to give up our quality, organic, grass-fed ingredients. I'll have to start cooking from scratch more than ever before and stick with the basics, bulk foods, and seasonal produce. It also means giving up animal products and moving toward a more plant-based diet. This will be excellent for our health and if the children need or want some occasional goat milk, fish, or meat, that is affordable and fine.

Our two kitchen gardens can produce plenty of free organic food. I'm already harvesting mustard greens, spinach, zucchini, and small tomatoes. If I keep rotating the crops, harvesting, and replanting, I can really feed my family for a little bit of labor and some seeds. I'm learning lots of useful information like learning to utilize small spaces and saving seeds from the foods we eat. I also plan on trying to plant fruit trees in pots from the seeds themselves. All of these skills will help us save even more money in the future.

I got the idea merely from my compost, tomato plants, and a lone avocado seed. I am careful about not having seeds in the compost but I'm sloppy with leftover tomato scraps, and now I have tomato plants growing all over the place: with the onions, in the side yards, with the zucchini, the melon . . . they're everywhere. It's the seeds from the compost. As for the healthiest and fastest-growing avocado tree? It was simply a pit from an avocado we used on our burgers one night. Bali threw it in the raised bed outside our laundry room and it has thrived.

Not too long ago, I was gifted a pressure canner and huge dehydrator by a wonderful woman. The same woman recently gave me more rain barrels, more containers, boxes of canning jars, a sealer, a hand-crank mill, *and* hard wheat berries! She's like my fairy godmother! I had just added some of these items to my Amazon wish list. She is also a Master Gardener, so she gives me the most fantastic advice on everything from trees, to gardens, and canning. I have everything, and I mean everything I need to be self-reliant.

But what does it mean to really cook from scratch and grow your own food? It ain't easy at first, sisters and brothers, but after a while, it gets easier as we learn from mistakes and practice, practice, practice.

It's like running an organic food café that grows most of its own food. You must be on top of things always. Once you harvest one food, you immediately plant another, you have seedlings going in the greenhouse, you know the Farmers' Almanac growing schedule for your area, and you keep researching and educating yourself. At some point, you will be able to relax because you'll be so good at it, you could do it in your sleep.

Then there is cooking from scratch, canning your own food from the garden, and keeping a pantry stocked and rotated so you don't eat anything rancid. It means prepping and cooking ahead, making dry batches of mixes for the shelves, and casseroles for the freezer. When you truly cook from scratch you can't just whip something up; it takes time, so if you have hungry children this can mean drama.

I asked Bali to put in his notice on Saturday. Sunday, I rested. Monday, I wrote out our complete budget. Tuesday, I processed it all and found free mulch on Craigslist. We drove all the way to Sacramento and loaded up the truck. Today, I cooked a lot of food since we didn't have anything quick and easy to make. I find that a big pot of beans, a loaf of bread, a pan of cornbread, a huge pan of baked potatoes, and a batch of homemade granola is a good start.

And off we go!

If I Were Poor...

I don't mean to get into poverty consciousness, but for some odd reason, I'm almost too fascinated with how to live on very little and still have an amazing existence. I grew up seeing my mother struggle with money. However, we always had a nice home. I wore a lot of hand-me-downs but I really loved getting bags of clothes that were new to me. We ate good, healthy food, as my mother was a decent cook and knew how to feed us through lean times. I only knew that we had times when money was a whimsical idea because my mother fretted and was constantly working the figures in her head (out loud). But this was her own doing, being poor at times. She was awful with money and never had a solid budget and she didn't save for those lean times. When she had money, she would quickly spend it all on a home renovation project, instead of being happy with what we had and doing little projects that were affordable and would make the place cozier.

I play poor in theory. We are a family of four and live on around $30K to $35K a year in Northern California. For some, this would be a struggle but through wise choices and thinking ahead, we live luxuriously on this sum. But I pretend that we have no money because it ensures that we will always have plenty in the long run. I pretend that we have no money to buy anything, unless it is something that will improve the quality of our lives.

For example, we took the smallest mortgage loan we were offered and made do. It wasn't easy, and we searched far and wide for a home to purchase. We were outbid many times and it looked hopeless. My husband pleaded with me to wait just a little bit longer until he had two years of employment under his belt, at which time the bank would approve us for a larger loan. But I refused. I loved the challenge (even though I did cry in my coffee a couple of times) and I wanted a tiny mortgage. Why buy a house unless we will save money by paying less on a mortgage than we did on rent?

I also wanted a mortgage that was so small that if hard times hit – I mean *really* hard times – Bali could work bagging groceries or flipping burgers and still pay the mortgage and bills, allowing me to stay home with our children.

I try to get our utility bills as low as possible, we had solar installed, switched to a new gas company, use our extra water as graywater for the garden, and cut the cable. Making homemade cleaners and using rags and cloths to clean and wash dishes saves a lot of money. Buying in bulk, cooking from scratch, and having potatoes, rice, and beans as the foundation of our dishes saves hundreds of dollars. Using a stovetop percolator that doesn't require filters, a vacuum that doesn't require bags, and a mop with a cloth head that can be washed is another money saver.

We go out when there are a few extra coins in the money jar. We will have a slice of pizza at Whole Foods because it's the best, or buy a box of reduced day-old vegan cookies at the health food store. We don't mind not going out to dinner as we are usually disappointed with the fare and I lament the loss of $50 or more that could have been used to stock my pantry instead.

I am no seamstress nor am I able to knit nice sweaters for the kiddies, but I can plant food. I have two large kitchen gardens in my front and backyard. We pulled up the 70-year-old lawn and improved the soil with free homemade compost and horse manure we got from some horse stables a few miles away. We planted 16 fruit and nut trees and even some grapes. The organic produce bounty increases each year and our grocery bill decreases.

I save all sorts of metal coffee cans and large tomato cans. These can be used for plants, pen holders, storage, baking, and can be decorated by the craftier soul.

If I were truly poor this is how I would live:

I would rent or buy a super cheap house. I frankly don't care if it's a cabin or trailer so long as it's suitable and can be improved with some painting and scrubbing. A can of paint can do wonders on the appearance of old, ugly walls. You can check the paint and hardwood stores for "oops paint." This is what they usually call paint that was returned because the color was simply not right for someone, or the store made a mistake when mixing it. A good cleaning can also make all the difference. I would plant all around the house with flowers and gardens.

I would dig up whatever land I had, be it a small or large yard, and buy seeds at Dollar Tree (four to five bags for $1) or find places I could use food stamps to buy fruit and nut trees, seeds, herb plants, and so on. You can even save seeds and pits from your own produce and plant those. We grew a tree from an avocado pit that we saved from dinner one night. I had the most successful and abundant tomato plant that grew from tomato seeds in the compost, probably from a salad. You could just save every seed, and start from there. It can be an apple, avocado, lemon, tomato, cucumber, or whatever you want. Look up gardening sites and check YouTube to find ways to grow these things. If I lived in an apartment, I'd plant my seeds in pots in the front or on the patio. I'd plant trees from seeds in big containers to take with me when I had land of my own. A tree from seed takes years to bear fruit, so I would have time to transplant. I would ask neighbors if I could have some trimmings from geraniums to plant in my front yard or for pots on my stoop or porch.

I would save all my tin cans, large and small, to plant trees, plants, produce, and to bake cakes and bread, and decorate my home with. I would save store-bought plastic containers and produce bags to store my food in.

I would hope for a wood floor so that I only needed a broom, and I would use a pot and rag to wash my floors. Vinegar and a little dish soap are all one needs for cleaning everything from windows and mirrors to floors. Baking soda is a good scrub and deodorizer. I would plant a lemon tree, as lemons are not only great for lemonade on hot days, but they are also great for cleaning.

I would take free ROP (Regional Occupational Program) classes through my college to learn new skills. With a BOGW (Board of Governors Fee Waiver) and financial aid, I could afford to do it. With ROP, I could take the classes at my own pace, thus eliminating the stress of deadlines, classes, and a schedule that might be hard on me.

I would join a church or spiritual center for community and activities to be involved in, have spiritual food, and many other things that would be fun, good for my family, and free or low cost.

I would learn to mend our clothes and keep them nice as long as possible. I would find a rope, make a clothesline, and hang my clothes to dry to save on the electric and gas bill, making clothes last longer. I would learn to knit blankets and find yarn at garage sales or free on Craigslist. I would use them on our sofa and to keep the kids warm during winter.

To decorate my home, I would go to nice neighborhoods and search the streets on garbage night, or check yard sales after people are just getting rid of the last of their goods for free or at very cheap prices. I would wait for big sales at thrift stores. I would search the Free section of Craigslist and FreelyWheely. I would accept hand-me-downs no matter what, so people got the word that I was open to receiving. I would ask for trimmings from house plants, then root them and grow my own.

Dollar Tree has some good things for cheap. They have kitchen utensils, clothespins, garden seeds, tablecloths, and hair clips. I'm not a big fan but it can be a useful store if used right.

I would cook from scratch and mostly, if not all, vegetarian. I would drink water and pass the dairy sections. My food would consist of simple, clean, whole foods. I'd buy and eat the cheapest beans, lentils, rice, and potatoes. Pintos are the cheapest beans and brown rice is typically cheaper than white. I would always try to buy in bulk, buy produce in season, and use the Dirty Dozen and Clean 15 list as a guide for organics.

I would treat myself to coffee at church events. I would go to free park concerts and volunteer at soup kitchens to get a free daily meal. I would make use of food pantries if money was super tight and I had a family to feed. I would get the help I needed and work on improving myself and my skills to build a better life for us all.

I would use things sparingly, save every penny, and look for ways to save all the time.

I would go without Internet and have a very cheap cell or house phone; probably just a house phone. I would love not having distractions or being plugged into the dramas of others or the world. I would maybe not even have a TV. I would just find a cheap radio for the kitchen to listen to local stations while I cleaned and cooked. If I did have a TV, I'd only have an antenna for local stations. I would love an excuse to not have all the modern gadgets, to spend my days peacefully working on the home or garden, and slowly building a little life for me and my family.

I would cook simple but nutritious foods, Depression Era style, with lots of fried potatoes and onions, baked beans, and homemade bread. I would make wacky cakes, and use good stuff like bacon just for flavoring the greens from our garden.

I would save up for jars and equipment to can my own food and I would find farms I could pick from for pennies or glean for free after harvest. I would ask people with fruit trees who let their fruit just rot on the branch if I could pick some fruit in exchange for a few dollars. Or perhaps, in exchange I would clean up the rotten fruit on the ground so that they wouldn't have to when they mowed. I would ask stores to give me old produce that they just throw away. I would go to coffee houses and collect old coffee grounds for my garden. I would build my pantry from huge sales on dented cans and boxed foods that are still fine to eat. I would search out every sale for food, clothes, or anything we needed.

For extra money, I might rent an extra room (if I had one) to a good person, or I would babysit for side money. I might do some housecleaning or dog walking any chance I got. I would fix up old furniture with a cheap can of spray paint, and dye old clothes to make them look new.

The library would be a great source for everything. I would get books, magazines, and use their computers. Maybe I would have an old VCR and buy $0.25 movies at yard sales and thrift stores.

The community college and the library are two places where I would spend a lot of time.

Even poor, one can have a good life. You can homestead anywhere and anytime. You can build a sweet nest with some cleaning and creativity. You could even dumpster dive. It's not my thing, but it works for others. You don't need much to be content. The more things I cut out, the more pleasant life becomes. All that "stuff" is really just distractions that create the desire for more and more, an insatiable pit that is unfillable by material things.

I love our life as it is but sometimes, I wonder what it would be like without the Internet and cell phones. What would it be like to just tidy and garden, simmer soups, and commune with God and nature all day à la Connie Hultquist? Yes, I can create this but as long as we can afford it, we have the extras. My husband would not be fine with cutting out the connection to the outside world.

However, there are many ways that I have created a simple and humble life in town, and turn to an older generation to find ways to live quietly and without all the hustle and bustle. This way of living also promotes huge savings and preparation for when times do get lean and mean, and if they do, you will sail right through, unscathed.

Chapter 13

Home Cooking

These are recipes from many of my books. Some are my own little dishes and many are from YouTube cooking channels. Others have been found online. There is something for everyone here: the simple cook, the vegetarian, the down-home cook . . . These are my favorite and frequently cooked dishes. They are money-saving, nourishing, filling, and delicious!

Peasant Bread

Ingredients

3 cups warm water

2 Tbsp yeast

5 cups white flour (you can substitute a cup for bran or flax)

2 or more cups wheat flour

Directions

In a large bowl, add 3 cups warm water (not *too* warm or it will kill the yeast) and sprinkle yeast in.

Add 5 cups white flour or 3 to 4 cups and 1 to 2 cups flax, bran, or whatever sounds good to you.

Stir, cover with a damp cloth, and let sit and rise for 1 hour.

Once risen, add the additional 2 cups of wheat flour and stir.

Pour onto a floured surface and knead it until it is no longer sticky. You may have to add more flour as you go.

Put back in the bowl and cover with the damp cloth. Let rise for another hour.

After the second rise, punch down and divide in half. Place each half into bread pans. Cover again for a third rise.

Bake in the oven at 350 degrees Fahrenheit

for 35 to 50 minutes.

This recipe is very adaptable. You can add anything to change it. Some examples: nuts, dried raisins and cinnamon, butter and honey (that is what the original recipe calls for), or make it super healthy with all sorts of oat bran and wheat bran.

Amish White Bread (source: www.allrecipes.com)

Ingredients

2 cups warm water

2/3 cups sugar

1 ½ Tbsp active dry yeast

1 ½ tsp salt

¼ cup oil

6 cups white flour

Directions

In a large bowl, mix water and yeast and let sit for about 5 minutes.

Add sugar, oil, salt, and flour last.

Mix and pour out onto floured surface and knead until no longer sticky (may need to add more flour).

Return to bowl and cover with damp cloth and let rise for 1 hour.

Once risen, punch down and divide in half.

Make into loaves and put into pans.

Cover with damp cloth again and let rise once more.

Bake at 350 degrees Fahrenheit for 30 to 40 minutes.

Tortillas (source: www.tasteofhome.com)

Ingredients

2 cups white flour (you can use half wheat, if you'd like)

½ teaspoon salt

¾ cup water

3 Tbsp oil

Directions

In a large bowl, add all ingredients.

Mix and knead, adding more flour or water if necessary. Let sit for 20 minutes.

Make into small balls and roll out onto a floured surface.

In a large skillet, cook tortillas over medium heat for approximately 1 minute on each side, or until lightly brown.

Keep and serve warm.

Mushroom Stroganoff (source: *Simply Sara Kitchen* on YouTube)

Ingredients

1 lb. button mushrooms, sliced (or any kind you prefer or whatever's on sale)

1 onion, diced

2 Tbsp olive oil

2 Tbsp butter

4 cloves minced garlic

1 Tbsp Worcestershire sauce

4 Tbsp white flour

3 cups vegetable stock

½ cup sour cream

¼ tsp thyme

Salt to taste

Granulated or powdered garlic to taste

Granulated or powdered onion to taste

Black pepper to taste

Directions

Sauté mushrooms and diced onions in the butter and oil until all the liquid from the mushrooms has cooked down/evaporated.

Add garlic and Worcestershire sauce and sauté for about a minute.

Sprinkle in the white flour, cook, and stir a couple more minutes.

Add vegetable stock, stir.

Add all seasonings: salt, garlic powder, onion powder, pepper, and thyme.

Simmer on low heat and add sour cream.

This is so delicious over egg noodles. I eat too many helpings. Sometimes I double the batch, we love it so much. Hands down, this recipe is one of my favorites!

Spaghetti with French Bread

Ingredients

1 loaf French bread (or you can bake your own)

1 lb. spaghetti pasta

2 (29 oz) cans Hunt's tomato sauce

1 lb. package grass-fed ground beef

Italian seasoning to taste

A few tablespoons of olive oil (or whichever kind you prefer or have in your pantry)

Granulated or powdered garlic to taste

Granulated or powdered onion to taste

Salt to taste

Directions

Sauté ground beef in pan with a little oil.

Add about 1 teaspoon each of garlic powder, onion powder, and Italian seasoning to the beef and cook until no longer pink or raw. You can drain the oil if you'd like, I usually do not.

Add Hunt's tomato sauce and add more garlic, onion, Italian seasoning, and salt to taste.

Simmer on very low for an hour.

Toward the end, cook pasta according to package directions, adding some olive oil and salt to the boiling water to prevent stickiness.

Serve sauce over pasta and add a nice hunk of French bread on the side.

Tuna Casserole

Ingredients

1 bag egg noodles

1 can tuna

1 can cream of mushroom

1 can cream of chicken

1 Tbsp chicken bouillon

1 ½ cups milk (add more if it seems too thick)

2 cups grated cheddar cheese, or use what you prefer or have on hand

Directions

In a large pan, simmer milk, tuna, cream of mushroom, cream of chicken, and chicken bouillon (this is your sauce).

Next, boil pasta until al dente.

Put pasta in a casserole dish and pour sauce over it.

Sprinkle cheese on top.

Bake for about 35 minutes at 350 degrees Fahrenheit.

You can double or triple this recipe to feed a larger family. I double this for the four of us and to have lunch to pack for my husband.

Vegan Pizza

Ingredients

Pizza dough (recipe follows)

Spaghetti sauce or tomato sauce

Daiya mozzarella cheese (vegan alternative)

Canned black olives without pits

Tomatoes

Bell pepper

Red onions

Any other vegetables you like

Dough (source: www.chef-in-training.com, but I've simplified it)

Ingredients

2 cups warm water

1 Tbsp yeast

1 Tbsp salt (optional)

5 cups flour

Directions

Mix yeast with water and let it sit for 10 minutes.

Add flour and mix, pour out onto floured surface and knead, adding more flour if necessary.

Make into a ball and return to bowl, cover with a kitchen towel and let rest for up to 20 minutes.

Divide into two parts, roll into a ball and roll out for your pizza.

Slice vegetables thinly and chop up olives.

Spread sauce with the back of a spoon and sprinkle a thin layer of vegan cheese.

Layer on vegetables.

Bake for 14 minutes at 400 degrees Fahrenheit, or until pizza is light brown and bubbly.

Briar Rabbit Burritos (This is a Briar Patch Co-op vegan vegetable wrap)

With this one you can add or omit any vegetables you like and use vegan mayo, cream cheese (vegan or dairy), or hummus.

Ingredients

Large tortillas (wheat, white flour, or flavored such as tomato basil, spinach, etc.)

Mayo, hummus, and/or cream cheese (vegan or not)

Sprouts

Bell peppers

Tomatoes

Shredded carrots

Peppers

Spinach or lettuce

Cucumbers

Pickles

Directions

Lay out the tortilla and spread on the hummus, mayo, or cream cheese.

Add vegetables (any vegetable you like or that is in season) in layers and add salt and pepper to taste.

Roll up like a burrito, cut in half, and devour.

Cooking Rice

If you have a rice cooker it is simply two parts water to one-part rice (white or brown). If you have no rice cooker, then add rice and water to a pot and cover, simmer on low for around 20 minutes for white rice and 40 minutes for brown.

I like to add chicken bouillon to flavor my rice. You can add butter, herbs, and other seasonings. Knorr soup packages make it a bit Rice-A-Roni-ish.

Large Pans of Delicious Veggies

Ingredients

Garlic

Red or yellow onions

Bags of frozen vegetables of your choice

Olive oil (or whichever kind you prefer or have in your pantry)

Salt and pepper

Method

These vegetables can be cooked in a regular pan, or you can use a cast iron pan, if you have one. If you use the latter, heat the pan slowly and then add plenty of oil and heat that slowly as well.

Slice a few cloves of garlic and slice up a whole onion and add both to the pan and sauté until onions are beginning to brown a bit.

Add frozen vegetables and sauté for as long as it takes to heat through.

I stir now and then and don't fret it they look a bit grilled.

I love using the mixed vegetables with peas, corn, green beans and carrots, and a bag of various green beans, wax beans and carrots.

Serve over rice.

You can add a little Veri Veri Teriyaki or any sauce, gravy, or eat as is. I also love this with macaroni and cheese. I just serve it side by side. So delicious and filling.

Baked Potato Fries

This method is a bit healthier than frying in oil.

Ingredients

Potatoes of your choice (we prefer Idaho russets)

Oil

Seasoning of your choice (garlic, salt, French fry seasoning, etc.)

Method

Wash and slice up your potatoes into steak fries' sizes.

Toss with some oil and spread out on cookie sheets.

Sprinkle seasonings.

Bake at 400 degrees Fahrenheit for approximately 30 minutes.

They won't cook evenly, so just keep checking and when they are golden on the edges, taste one.

Slow Cooker Pot Roast

Ingredients

1 package of roasting meat, approximately 3-4 pounds

1 can cream of mushroom

1 packet of onion soup mix

5-6 potatoes chopped into small chunks

5-6 carrots chopped into small chunks

Any other vegetables you like (I love to use frozen corn and peas)

Directions

In a slow cooker, add everything plus enough water to cover.

Cook on low for 6-8 hours, or on high for 4-6 hours.

I usually double this recipe and have plenty for a couple days' worth of lunches and dinners.

Vegan Garden Pie (knockoff of Shepherd's pie, but my way)

Ingredients

1 can mushroom gravy, or any gravy (sometimes I use cream of mushroom as well)

1 package of Lightlife Smart Ground Crumbles or textured vegetable protein (TVP) sautéed in vegetable broth

1 lb. bag of frozen peas and corn

½ onion, diced

Potatoes or potato flakes

Soy milk

Vegan butter

Oil

1 tsp garlic powder

1 tsp onion powder

Salt and pepper to taste

Directions

In a large skillet, sauté onions in a bit of oil for about 5 minutes, or until translucent.

Add crumbles or the reconstituted TVP.

Add gravy and a bag of frozen vegetables and cook until heated through.

Next, add the garlic and onion powder, salt and pepper.

In a separate pot, boil potatoes, then drain, mash, add butter, salt and soy milk.

You can also just boil water to make your powdered potatoes and cook according to package directions.

Spread potatoes on top of meat substitute and vegetable mixture and put in the oven to bake for 35 minutes at 350 degrees Fahrenheit.

I always double this recipe.

Minestrone Soup (source: *Simply Sara Kitchen* on YouTube)

Ingredients

2 Tbsp oil

2 Tbsp butter

1 onion, chopped

2 stalks celery, chopped

2 to 3 zucchinis, chopped

4 tomatoes, chopped

4 to 5 cloves garlic, minced

1 (15 oz) can cannellini beans

1 (15 oz) can kidney beans

1 (15 oz) can black beans

4 cups water

1 cup frozen green beans

Handful of shredded carrots

1 Tbsp tomato paste

3 cups tomato juice

2 Tbsp vegetable bouillon

2 tsp parsley

1 tsp oregano

1 tsp basil

½ tsp thyme

Salt and pepper to taste

1 bag fresh spinach

Chunk of parmesan cheese

1 ¼ cup pasta shells

Directions

In a large skillet, sauté butter, oil, onion, celery, zucchini, and tomatoes.

Add garlic and cook for 1 minute.

Drain canned beans and add to skillet.

Add water, green beans, carrots, tomato paste, tomato juice, bouillon, herbs, salt, and pepper.

Stir well.

Add a few pieces of parmesan cheese and let it simmer for a while.

Add 1 ¼ cup pasta shells and cook until tender, about 7 minutes.

Next, add a bagful of fresh spinach.

This soup is SO delicious! It really does taste like Olive Garden's version, or better.

Potato and/or Salad Bar

This is for those days when you want filling, healthy food but in a self-serve style. I just bake up potatoes, shred a huge bowl of lettuce and put out small bowls and containers of whatever you would put on a salad or potato along with bottles of dressings and sauces. You can have anything you fancy, but here are some ideas for toppings:

For potatoes:

Sour cream

Butter

Chives

Cheese

Canned chili

Tomatoes

Broccoli

Cheese sauce

For salad:

Tomatoes

Canned kidney and/or garbanzo beans

Onions

Olives

Cucumbers

Sprouts

Cheese

Cabbage

Garbage Salad

Ingredients

Lettuce

Shredded carrots

Kidney beans

Tomatoes, chopped

Onions, chopped

Olives, chopped

Ground beef or turkey, cooked and cooled (optional)

Homemade ranch dressing with taco seasoning mixed in

Shredded cheddar cheese

Nacho Cheese Doritos (or Fritos Corn Chips, if you prefer)

Method

Shred a huge bowl of lettuce and add everything but the dressing and cheese until the very last moment. Crumble chips on top.

This was a friend's recipe, but I think many know this one. I turned it into a bit of a nacho salad. I love making the packets of ranch using whole fat buttermilk and mayo. Then I add packet taco seasoning to taste.

Punjabi Bean or Lentil Soup (Bali's recipe)

If you learn to make these sautés you can make all sorts of bean and lentil soups. You can also cook meats in these sautés.

Ingredients

1 pound of any kind of beans or lentils, dry

1 onion (red or yellow)

1 pepper (we use mild peppers)

3 or more cloves of garlic

1-ounce fresh ginger

2 tomatoes, chopped

1 cup fresh cilantro, chopped

1 tsp coriander seeds

1 tsp cumin seeds

1 tsp turmeric

1 Tbsp masala seasoning (There are masalas for beans and meats. They are small boxes of mixed seasonings you can find in the Indian foods section of the grocery store or at Indian food stores. You can even find them on www.amazon.com.)

Oil

Salt and pepper to taste

Directions

In a large pot, add washed beans or lentils of choice.

Add water until there are two inches of water above the beans/lentils and begin to simmer on medium heat.

Add turmeric.

Chop up all the vegetables and add half an onion and one tomato to the soup in the beginning.

Add half a teaspoon of pepper and full teaspoon of salt, about a teaspoon of oil, and a few minced cloves of garlic.

In a skillet add a tablespoon of oil, coriander and cumin, and toast for a minute or two.

Next, add remaining garlic, onions, tomatoes, and peppers.

Sauté for about 2-3 minutes.

Add a heaping teaspoon of masala, then sauté and cook for a few more minutes, or until vegetables are soft.

Add cooked vegetable mixture to pot of cooked beans or lentils.

Add cilantro at the end.

Peanut Butter Cookies (source: www.myrecipes.com)

I love this recipe because it's cheap. I always have the ingredients on hand, and it takes just minutes.

Ingredients

1 cup peanut butter

1 cup sugar

1 egg

1 tsp vanilla extract

(Nuts, raisins, and chocolate chips are all optional)

Directions

Mix all ingredients and spoon globs onto a cookie sheet, about two inches apart.

Bake for 10 to 15 minutes at 325 degrees Fahrenheit.

I always double the batch!

Easiest Cheesecake Ever

This is a no bake, super easy, and so good recipe. I have no idea where I got it from.

Ingredients

1 store bought graham cracker crust

8 oz cream cheese

1/3 cup sugar

2 tsp vanilla extract

1 cup sour cream

Directions

Use a beater to mix cream cheese, sugar, vanilla extract, and sour cream.

Pour into graham cracker pie crust.

Chill in fridge for at least 4 hours to allow it to set.

Homemade Sugar-Free Lemonade

Ingredients

Water

Lemons

Stevia (you can also use real sugar, honey, or maple syrup, but then it won't be sugar-free)

Method

In a pitcher filled with water, add as much squeezed lemon juice and Stevia as you like.

Keep adding sweetener and lemon juice until it tastes yummy.

Moon Beam Tea (source: *The Help Yourself Cookbook for Kids: 60 Easy Plant-Based Recipes Kids Can Make to Stay Healthy and Save the Earth* by Ruby Roth)

Ingredients

Hot water

Chamomile tea

Honey, agave, or sugar

Milk or plant milk

Method

Brew tea in hot water.

Add sweetener and milk of choice to taste.

The kids love this tea and I drink it at night.

Cranberry Water

Ingredients

Water

Cranberry juice

Ice

Method

Add 1-part cranberry juice to 3 parts water.

Serve over ice.

This is a great way to get kids to drink more water in the summer. I usually use pure cranberry juice without sugar and add Stevia to it.

Homemade Yogurt

Ingredients

1 gallon of milk

1 cup of yogurt (you can use some from your previous batch or buy at the store if you are just starting out)

Directions

Add milk to a large Dutch oven or any pot with a tight-fitting lid.

Simmer slowly until temperature reaches 200 degrees Fahrenheit.

Remove from heat and let cool to 115

degrees Fahrenheit.

Turn oven on to preheat for about 10 minutes.

In a separate bowl, combine 2 cups of heated milk with 1 cup of yogurt.

Whisk gently and add back to Dutch oven or pot and stir to combine.

Place in turned off oven and leave overnight.

If it doesn't firm up, let sit for a few more hours. The house and/or oven must be warm. This allows it to solidify with all the good bacteria and cultures. This is so healthy, and the cost is $1 for a big container instead of $5 or more for organic yogurt at the grocery store.

Vegan Chocolate Cake (this sounds funky, but it is better than regular cake)

Ingredients

2 ½ cups white flour

¾ cup to 1 cup cocoa

2 tsp salt

2 tsp baking soda

2 cups honey

1 cup coconut oil

1 cup water

1 cup almond milk or soy milk

2 tsp vanilla extract (you can substitute and use any other preferred extract such as maple, coconut, etc.)

Directions

Preheat oven to 350 degrees Fahrenheit.

In a large bowl, mix together flour, cocoa, salt, and baking soda.

Add honey, coconut oil, water, milk, and vanilla extract.

Mix until combined.

Pour into a 9-inch cake pan and bake for 35 minutes, or until toothpick inserted in the center comes out clean.

Frosting

Ingredients

4 oz dark chocolate (you can use milk chocolate, but then it won't be vegan)

2 Tbsp coconut oil

1/3 cup water

Directions

In a medium saucepan, add chocolate, coconut oil, and water.

On low to medium heat, stir frequently until melted. Pour on top of cake.

Whole Wheat Pizza Crust

Ingredients

1 tsp sugar

1 ½ cups warm water

1 Tbsp active dry yeast

1 Tbsp olive oil

1 tsp salt

2 cups whole wheat flour

1 ½ cups white flour

Directions

In a large bowl, dissolve sugar in warm water.

Sprinkle yeast on top.

Let stand for 10 minutes.

Stir in olive oil, salt, whole wheat flour, and 1 cup of white flour.

Pour out onto clean, floured surface and knead in remaining white flour until dough becomes smooth.

Place in oiled bowl, lightly coating dough.

Cover with towel and let stand for 1 hour.

After 1 hour, your dough should be doubled. Place dough on floured surface and divide into two parts.

Form into tight balls and let rise for 45 more minutes.

Oil pizza pans. Roll out and stretch to fit pans and load with desired sauce and toppings.
I just use Hunt's tomato sauce with extra garlic powder and Italian seasoning as my sauce.

Bake at 425 degrees Fahrenheit for 14 to 20 minutes. Yummy.

Mom's Spaghetti Sauce (this was my mother's sauce from what I remember, with a few things added or taken out)

Ingredients

Hunt's cans of tomato sauce (very

inexpensive)

Ground beef

Ground pork sausage

Green bell pepper, finely chopped

Italian seasoning

Freshly chopped garlic or

granulated/powdered garlic

Directions

In a large pot, brown meat until fully cooked.

Add sauce, bell pepper, and seasonings.

Simmer on low heat for about an hour or so.

The longer it simmers on very low heat, the more flavorful the sauce. You can make your own tomato sauce, as well.

Homemade Tomato Sauce (This is from *Dump Dinners*, with some added ingredients)

Ingredients

Tomatoes (very ripe)

Onions

Salt

Butter

Italian seasoning

Garlic

Directions

In a large pot, simmer for one hour.

When cooled, blend and store in refrigerator.

Vegetarian Black Bean Enchiladas

This is my own little creation. This dish is so good!

Ingredients

Black beans, homemade or store-bought

White rice, cooked with chicken bouillon, preferably

Cheese (mild cheddar, jalapeno cheddar, or cotija)

Corn tortillas

Green enchilada sauce, canned

Butter

Directions

In a large skillet, heat up a stack of corn tortillas with a touch of butter, until they are soft and pliable. Set aside.

Grease a casserole pan.

Have all three cheeses shredded and mixed on a big plate.

Place tortillas side by side in pan.

Fill with beans and cheese and roll.

Arrange side by side.

When pan is full, sprinkle cheese and pour the can of enchilada sauce on top. Sprinkle more cheese.

Bake at 350 degrees Fahrenheit for 35 to 40 minutes.

Serve with white rice and beans on the side. You can use plain water or vegetable stock to cook the rice, if you prefer. Yahoo, it's good!

Frozen Bean and Cheese Burritos

Ingredients

Pinto or black beans, cooked

Rice, cooked

Cheese

Tortillas

Butter (optional)

Directions

In a big pot, mix desired amount of rice, beans, shredded cheese, and any seasonings you like. Granulated garlic and onion work great here.

When everything is mixed well and cheese is melted, scoop into a large tortilla and fold to make burritos. Avoid overfilling.

Place all burritos seam side down on a greased cookie sheet.

Lightly brush tops with melted butter.

Bake at 350 degrees Fahrenheit for 20 to 25 minutes, or until golden brown.

Be sure to keep an eye on them so they don't burn.

Enjoy and freeze the rest.

These are delicious, much better than the store bought (because they have substantial amounts of beans and rice), and you can just take one or two out of the freezer and microwave to reheat. I make tons at a time.

Down-Home Chicken Soup

Ingredients

3-5 lbs. bone-in chicken (whole, thighs, or legs)

Vegetables (all kinds)

Chicken bouillon

Italian seasoning or a combination of basil and oregano

Salt

½ lb. egg noodles or pasta, cooked (rice or barley are fine, too)

Directions

Place chicken in a large pot.

Add water to cover.

Cook on low to medium heat for 1 ½ to 2

hours, or until internal temperature reaches 165 degrees Fahrenheit.

Once cool enough to handle, transfer chicken to platter to debone.

Return to pot, add bouillon, seasonings, and salt to taste.

Simmer for approximately 15-20 minutes more.

Add desired vegetables and continue to simmer until they are soft.

Add cooked egg noodles or pasta and serve.

You may use rice or barley instead. Pasta and rice get mushy in soup after some time. Egg noodles are the best for this soup. You can also just use chicken and vegetables and serve with some freshly baked bread.

Atta Flatbread

Ingredients

2 cups Atta flour

1 cup water

3-4 Tbsp butter

This is what I call an Indian tortilla.

Directions

In a large bowl, add the flour and water and mix to form a dough.

Make into small balls.

On a floured surface, roll out each one.

Add a pat of butter (approximately ½ tablespoon) to hot pan.

Cook each flatbread for about 30-45 seconds per side. Serve warm.

Wheat and white Atta flour can be found at Indian grocery stores, the international foods aisle at some grocery stores, and online. Buy a big bag and keep it on hand for these delicious flatbreads.

We eat this with everything. His curry chicken, my black beans.

Cheap and Easy Snack Ideas

Snacking is fun and can be nutritious, so I like to make healthy snack plates. Sometimes my kids and I just graze throughout the day and then eat a proper meal in the evening with Bali.

- Cheese and raisins
- Homemade raw granola bars made with oats, nuts, seeds, nut butters, and raisins (great recipes can be found online)
- Olives and pickles
- Organic yogurt loaded with probiotics (try plain Greek and add berries or make your own)
- Sliced and/or chopped fruit with nut butters
- Vegetables with peanut butter or hummus
- Seeds, nuts, and dried fruit
- Popcorn with coconut oil, nutritional yeast, and salt
- Homemade sliced bread with jam, nut butters, or cheese
- Sprouts
- Shredded carrots and red cabbage with a little ranch or dressing of your choice

- Salad (most kids like salad and if they say they don't, just keep serving it, trying different dressings, and they will eventually)

Homemade Convenience Foods

Make your own versions of frozen convenience foods! I like to make frozen lasagnas and enchiladas, bean, rice, and cheese burritos, and so much more. Just cook a double or triple batch of lasagna, burritos, soup, or casseroles, and freeze the extra.

Substitutions for Name Brand Convenience Foods (some of these recipes are from *The Complete Tightwad Gazette*)

Cocoa Mix

Ingredients

10 cups powdered milk

6 oz non-dairy creamer

1 lb. Nestle Nesquik Chocolate Milk Powder

1/3 cup confectioners' sugar

Directions

Mix well. Store in airtight container in a cool, dry place.

Shake 'n Bake (remember this oldie, but goodie?)

Ingredients

4 cups flour

4 cups crushed saltine crackers

4 Tbsp salt

2 tsp onion powder

3 Tbsp paprika

Directions

Mix well. Store in airtight container in a cool, dry place.

Raisin Oatmeal Scones

Ingredients

1 ½ cups flour

1 cup dry oatmeal

1 tsp baking soda

½ tsp salt

¼ cup margarine

½ cup raisins

¾ cup sour milk (milk with 2 tsp vinegar)

1 egg, beaten

Directions

Preheat oven to 400 degrees Fahrenheit.

In a large bowl, mix flour, oatmeal, baking soda, salt, margarine, raisins, and sour milk until all ingredients are combined.

Roll out to approximately 3/4 inch thick and cut into squares or shapes.

Place on large cookie sheet. Bake for 10 minutes.

Remove from oven, glaze with beaten egg, and bake for 5 more minutes, or until golden brown.

Seasoned Salt

Ingredients

8 Tbsp salt

3 Tbsp black pepper

2 Tbsp paprika

½ tsp onion powder

½ tsp garlic powder

Directions

Mix well. Store in airtight container in a cool, dry place.

Taco Seasoning

Ingredients

6 tsp chili powder

4 ½ tsp cumin

5 tsp paprika

3 tsp onion powder

2 ½ tsp garlic powder

¼ tsp cayenne pepper powder

Directions

Mix well. Store in airtight container in a cool, dry place.

Onion Soup Mix

Ingredients

¾ cup dried, minced onion

4 tsp onion powder

1/3 cup beef bouillon powder

¼ tsp ground celery seeds

¼ tsp sugar

Directions

Mix well. Store in airtight container in a cool, dry place.

Seasoned Rice Mix

Ingredients

3 cups uncooked rice

¼ cup dried parsley flakes

6 Tbsp chicken or beef bouillon powder

2 tsp onion powder

½ tsp garlic powder

½ tsp dried thyme

Directions

Mix well and store in airtight container in a cool, dry place.

Cook as you would normally cook rice.

Country Biscuit Mix

Ingredients

10 cups flour

⅓ cup baking powder

1 Tbsp salt

2 cups shortening

Directions

Using a food processor or pastry cutter, mix well to make sure shortening is evenly distributed.

Store in airtight container. Lasts 1 to 6 months at room temperature, during colder weather.

You may also refrigerate. Use it the same way you would use Bisquick.

Meatless Monday Casserole

Ingredients

3 cups vegetable broth

¾ cups uncooked lentils

½ cup uncooked brown rice

¾ cup onion, chopped

½ tsp sweet basil

¼ tsp oregano

¼ tsp thyme

¼ tsp garlic powder

1 ½ cups shredded cheese (use your favorite)

Directions

Add all ingredients (except cheese) to a baking dish and mix.

Cover and bake at 375 degrees Fahrenheit for approximately 1 ½ hours, stirring once halfway through the cooking time.

Sprinkle cheese and return to oven for an additional 10 minutes, or until it has melted and is golden and bubbly.

Remove from oven and let cool for another 10 minutes before serving.

A More Plant-Based Kitchen: How to Prepare Your Pantry for a Vegan or Plant-Based Life

Here are the foods I keep stocked on my shelves and in the refrigerator and freezer:

Dry goods

White flour
Wheat flour
Oats, old fashioned
Steel cut oats
Black beans
Pinto beans
Garbanzo beans
Brown lentils
Red lentils
Walnuts
Cashews
Almonds
Brown rice
White rice
Coffee
Nut butters
Black olives, canned (think pizza)

Baking Supplies

Baking powder
Baking soda
Ground cinnamon
Vanilla extract
Nutmeg
Ground ginger
Date syrup
Coconut sugar
Powdered sugar
Cacao powder (not to be confused with cocoa)
Maple syrup

Gluten-free mixes are also good to keep on hand if you have issues, or just prefer them. Bob's Red Mill makes gluten-free mixes for pancakes, pizza crust, cornbread, and more.

Seasonings and Sauces

Sriracha
Himalayan pink salt
Ground black pepper
Ground white pepper
Italian seasoning
Fennel powder
Cayenne powder
Tajin (with an added squeeze of lime juice, this is great on fruit)
Garlic powder
Onion powder
Turmeric
Masala
Nutritional yeast
Vinegars: white, rice, and wine
Coconut oil
Sesame oil
Olive oil

Frozen Goods

Lots of veggies and greens
Berries
Bananas
Quorn Meatless & Soy Free Turk'y Roast

Veggie burgers (Amy's, Boca, Quorn,
Gardein...so many to try!)
Veggie hot dogs
Hot dog buns
Hamburger buns

Refrigerator

Ketchup (Organicville is a good one)
Relish
Mustard
Coconut aminos
Greens
Vegetables
Fruit
Plant-based milks
Earth Balance butter or plant-based butters
Vegenaise
Annie's salad dressings (read the label, not all
are vegan)
Vegan ranch dressing (Follow Your Heart is
a good brand)
Hoisin Sauce
Vegetarian Worcestershire Sauce
Chili garlic sauce
Sweet chili sauce
Pickles (whole dill and sliced bread and
butter)
Olives (whatever you like, we love garlic
stuffed)

Baskets

Potatoes: Yukon Gold, Idaho russets, red, sweet, and purple
Tomatoes
Avocados
Ginger
Onions
Garlic
Lemons and limes

Delicious Vegan Dishes

Lentil Loaf (source: *High Carb Hannah* on YouTube)

This is delicious. I'm fond of real meatloaf, so I was sure this would not pass the test. It did. This lentil loaf with ketchup and mashed potatoes is a dream. Add some peas or corn to really make it a plateful of winter comfort food.

Ingredients

1 cup brown lentils

½ cup red lentils

1 ½ cups oat flour (just ground oats)

3 cups plus 6 Tbsp water

1 carrot, chopped

2 stalks celery, chopped

1 bell pepper, any color (I like green, and it's less pricey), diced

½ medium onion (red or yellow if you prefer), finely diced

1 Tbsp fennel powder

1 Tbsp Italian seasoning

1 Tbsp onion powder

3 Tbsp ground flax seeds

1 tsp cayenne (optional)

I like to add 1 Tbsp garlic powder and 1 Tbsp salt

Directions

In a medium to large pot, mix brown and red lentils with diced onion, celery, carrot, bell pepper, and 3 cups water.

Bring to boil.

Reduce heat to simmer until lentils are soft. It's okay if there is a little water but most should be evaporated. I'd say twenty to thirty minutes. I usually just keep an eye on it.

In a small bowl, mix ground flax seeds with 6 tablespoons of water. Let sit while the lentils and vegetables cook. This is going to get gelatinous and be your binder.

In a separate bowl, mix all the seasonings: fennel, Italian seasoning, garlic and onion powder, and salt if you like. You can even add pepper and other seasonings. Play with it.

Grind the oats in a blender to make the flour.

When lentils and vegetables are cooked, add the oat flour, seasonings, and flax mixture.

Mix well and divide. Form into loaves. Place into 2 nonstick pans.

Bake at 350 degrees Fahrenheit for approximately 30-45 minutes.

Note: After about 20 minutes, remove from oven, add about ¼ cup of ketchup to each loaf and return to oven to finish baking.

Makes 2 loaves.

Mashed Potatoes

Ingredients

Potatoes (any potato will do, but Yukon gold
is the richest and yummiest in this dish)

Plain, unsweetened soy milk

Vegan butter (optional)

Salt and pepper to taste

Nutritional yeast

Granulated or powdered onion

Granulated or powdered garlic

Method

In a large pot, boil potatoes until tender.

Drain and return to pot.

Add all remaining ingredients and use a hand

mixer to whip them to a creamy texture.

You can add even more seasonings if you're feeling daring.

Corn and Brussels Sprouts

My kids love this! I love this! You can substitute vegetable broth for the oil and butter.

Ingredients

Frozen corn

Fresh brussels sprouts

Earth Balance vegan butter

Coconut oil

Garlic

Salt

White pepper

Method

In a large pan, sauté garlic in coconut oil and butter. Don't toast or burn, just heat to release the essence of the garlic. Add frozen corn.

Wash and cut brussels sprouts in half and add to pan. Don't cook them too long.

Add more butter, salt and pepper. Serve.

Vegan Tostadas from Heaven

This dish is so easy and fast.

Ingredients

Homemade or canned refried beans (I sometimes add my favorite canned beans: Ranch Style Beans and S&W Chili Beans)

Tostadas

Lettuce

Tomatoes

Homemade vegan thousand island dressing

Sriracha

Method

I usually make refried beans and throw in a can of the S&W Chili and Ranch Style beans to make it fabulous. Mash it all up.

Top tostadas with beans, shredded lettuce, chopped tomatoes and then drizzle generously with thousand island dressing and Sriracha.

Homemade Vegan Thousand Island Dressing

I combined three different recipes here. There is Worcestershire sauce in mine, and that is not vegan (I was disappointed). But there is a vegan substitute, yay!

Ingredients

1 cup Vegenaise

1 Tbsp Annie's Worcestershire sauce (vegan, baby!)

2 Tbsp ketchup

1 Tbsp lemon juice (fresh)

2 Tbsp relish

1 Tbsp minced garlic (jarred is best for strong flavor)

1 Tbsp red onion, minced

Salt to taste

White pepper to taste

Vinegar is optional (I don't use it)

Directions

In a large bowl, mix all ingredients until combined.

Store in a jar and keep refrigerated.

It gets better each day, as the flavors marinate. I sort of eyeball the measurements and add to taste, so this is truly a foundation recipe. Experiment to make it to your liking. Add more lemon or pepper, if you wish. You can even spice it up with a little Sriracha.

Sometimes I just drizzle this dressing on lettuce leaves and eat them like an appetizer. I eat a head of lettuce almost daily.

Martha Stewart's One Pot Pasta

I used to make this when we used chicken broth and it was incredibly delicious. I now just use vegetable broth instead. The recipe calls for water, but I find that a broth makes it 10 times yummier.

Ingredients

12 oz linguine pasta

1 onion, chopped

½ tsp pepper flakes

2 Tbsp olive oil

4 ½ cups vegetable broth

12 oz cherry or grape tomatoes, chopped in half or quartered

4 cloves fresh garlic, minced

2 sprigs basil

Salt and pepper to taste

Directions

Place all ingredients in a pot and bring to a boil.

Reduce heat and stir occasionally until all the water or broth is absorbed by the pasta.

Stovetop Vegan Pizza

This dish is a combination of recipes. Both *High Carb Hannah* and Nikki over at www.chef-in-training.com have versions, but you may top it however you like. This dish works well with my gas stove; it seems easier to make, and I love the thick, pan style.

There are a few parts to this pizza.

The Perfect Pizza Dough (source: www.chef-in-training.com)

Ingredients

2 cups warm water

1 Tbsp active dry yeast

1 Tbsp salt

5 cups flour

Directions

Add yeast to warm water and let sit for 5 minutes.

Add half the flour and mix well, pour onto floured board and mix in remainder.

Knead and return to bowl to sit covered with a towel for 20 minutes.

She gets a bit fancier, but I find simple works as well.

Pizza Assembly

Method

Sprinkle cornmeal on bottom of a large skillet.

Press dough into the pan to completely cover the bottom.

Add sauce and toppings of your choice.

We love tons of olives, corn, red onions, and pineapple. Go easy on sliced tomatoes if you decide to use them, as they make the dough soggy. Be careful not to use too much sauce for this same reason.

If you would like a vegan cheese, *High Carb Hannah* has a good recipe for one:

Ingredients

¼ cup cashews

3 Tbsp nutritional yeast

½ Tbsp granulated or powdered garlic, or to taste

Himalayan pink salt, to taste

Directions

Blend all ingredients in a blender.

Sprinkle on pizza.

Place pan on stove and cover with a tight-fitting lid.

Cook on low for approximately 15 minutes. This part is tricky; sometimes it's taken up to 30 minutes if there are lots of watery toppings. Keep an eye on it.

When it is fully cooked, place it on a chopping board, cut and serve. So good.

Makes 2 pan pizzas.

Asian Noodle Soup

There is some controversy as to whether or not this is really considered vegan. I use a pho soup mix or wonton soup mix. The beef and chicken are artificial flavors and I've seen Rose from *Cheap Lazy Vegan* on YouTube eat artificially flavored chicken ramen. This is for you to decide. You can also just use an alternative vegan broth.

I just boil a huge pot of water with the soup seasoning, rice noodles, and tons of greens. Sometimes I get all this from our local Korean store, so I have no idea what the greens are called. We eat the soup in huge bowls that I also purchased there, and we use chopsticks because it's fun.

This is a great soup for cold days. You leave the table feeling warm, full, and fortified.

Packed Veggie Eggless Rolls

I make these now and then, and they are a hit, even with my elderly neighbors who love their meat. They are very high in fat, so this is a treat.

Ingredients

Egg roll wraps (get the soft, large ones)

Vegetables (red and green cabbage, carrots,

onions, bean sprouts)

Veri Veri Teriyaki

Oil (a light oil for frying)

Dipping sauce of choice (I use sweet chili

sauce)

Water for steaming

Directions

Shred vegetables in a food processor or grate and chop by hand. You can add whatever else you would like, such as tofu or other vegetables.

In a wok or large pan, add vegetables and a bit of water. Put the lid on to steam for a short period. You want the vegetables to be cooked, but still be a bit crunchy.

Drain, return to pan, and add Veri Veri Teriyaki sauce.

Lay the wrap on a dry surface and put a large amount of vegetables in the middle, then wrap it like a burrito and seal with a dab of water. I like to make batches, so they are fresh and crunchy.

In a large, deep pan, add about an inch of oil. Let the oil get hot, but not boiling, *crazy* hot.

Use tongs to carefully add egg rolls and turn as needed until golden brown.

Place on a platter with paper towels to absorb all the oil.

Serve with dipping sauce.

You can also choose different sauces, we just like Thai sweet chili sauce.

Faux Tuna Salad (source: www.revolutioninbloom.com)

1-15 oz can cooked garbanzo beans

½ cup diced dill pickles

½ cup diced celery

½ diced red onion

1 or 2 Tbsp nori sheets ground to flakes

Vegenaise (as much as you like)

Salt to taste

Pepper to taste

Add garbanzo beans to a food processor and pulse a few times, keeping them a bit textured, and not pasty. You want a sort of flaky texture. Pour into bowl.

Mix in all remaining ingredients and you're done.

I have taken to adding other things such as mustard and fresh lemon juice. Others like cayenne or other seasonings.

This recipe is very flexible. You can adjust all the ingredients to your liking; adding more of this, and less of that. I found we liked a ton of nori flakes and extra salt. This is a very good dish to eat on crackers and in sandwiches.

I usually double the batch.

Green Smoothie

Ingredients

Frozen bananas

Frozen berries (optional)

Almond or soy milk

Greens (best for smoothies are kale, spinach, dandelion greens, collards, and chard)

A Vitamix works best for these smoothies, but any good one will do.

Method

Start by blending the greens and milk.

Next, add bananas and frozen berries or any other fruit, one by one. Do this until it has reached the sweetness and creaminess you love.

Mangos and pineapple are good, too. You don't need to use all these greens in one smoothie.

Mix and match or just use one at a time.

Green Juice (Sometimes Red):

This recipe is very simple.

Ingredients

Apples

Fresh lemon, peeled

Fresh ginger, peeled

Cucumber

Carrots

Celery

Greens

Beets

Method

Juice all ingredients according to
manufacturer's directions.

You decide the amount of fruits and
vegetables you want to juice. We like to use
extra carrots and apples to make it a bit
sweeter for the kids. If you are trying to
detox from metals such as aluminum in
vaccines, throw in cilantro and parsley each
time.

Get the cheapest apples. When you juice
them, it doesn't matter if they are old. See if
your health food store marks down older
produce. Perhaps they are willing to give it

to you for compost. If so, take it home and then salvage what you can. My old co-op used to have boxes of reduced produce daily. I liked to buy bags of it and use it for juicing because even if it's bruised or funky, it all becomes juice.

Desserts and Coffee

What is life without sweets and coffee? Not much to me. Here are some vegan desserts, and one is even healthy! I'll also share my best coffee secrets.

Vegan Vanilla Cake (source: www.lovingitvegan.com)

Ingredients

1 ¾ cups all-purpose flour

1 cup sugar

1 tsp baking soda

½ tsp salt

1 cup plain soy milk

2 tsp vanilla extract

1/3 cup olive oil (I use coconut oil)

1 Tbsp white vinegar

Directions

In a large bowl, mix wet ingredients.

In another, mix dry ingredients.

Combine the two and pour in a baking pan. Bake in a preheated oven at 350 degrees Fahrenheit for 30 minutes or until toothpick inserted in the middle comes out clean.

Vegan Vanilla Buttercream Frosting
(source: www.elizabethrider.com)

Ingredients

1 cup Earth Balance butter

3 cups powdered sugar

2 tsp soy or almond milk

¾ tsp vanilla extract

Note: For chocolate buttercream I replace 1 cup of powdered sugar with 1 cup of cacao powder.

Directions

Whip until creamy.

Store in refrigerator in an airtight container for up to 7 days.

CHEF AJ's Black Bean Chocolate Brownies (source: *CHEF AJ* on YouTube)

These brownies are super healthy! I let my boys eat these some mornings for fun.

Ingredients

2 cups rinsed black beans, cooked

¾ cup oats (you can grind into flour or leave whole)

1 cup date syrup (I use Date Lady)

½ cup cocoa (I use cacao; it's healthier)

1 tsp baking powder

½ tsp baking soda

Chocolate chips, as little or as much as you

want (enjoy life!)

Directions

Place all ingredients in a food processor, pulse a few times, until combined. Pour into a baking pan. I like to use my cast iron skillet and then cover the top with dark chocolate chips. Sometimes I'll add sprinkles for fun. Bake in a preheated oven at 350 degrees Fahrenheit for 20-30 minutes, depending on the size of your pan.

Kate's Fancy Espresso Coffee

I don't drink this every day, or I'd have even more weight to lose.

Ingredients

Espresso

Milk

Water

Method

Make a strong cup of espresso in a stovetop Italian espresso maker. Pour into a large mug, add some hot water and a large scoop of Nature's Charm Sweetened Condensed Coconut Milk. This is a treat!

Use as much or as little espresso, water, and milk as you want.

I hope you enjoyed spending some time with me. Please visit us on YouTube at *Coffee With Kate.*

Printed in Great Britain
by Amazon